Kindred Sisters

New Testament Women Speak to Us Today

A Book of Meditation and Reflection

Dandi Daley Mackall

Augsburg
MINNEAPOLIS

This book is dedicated to the women of the Cinnamon Lake Bible Study.
Thanks for your help, prayers, and examples.

KINDRED SISTERS
New Testament Women Speak to Us Today

Copyright © 1996 Dandi Daley Mackall

Scripture quotations are from the New Revised Standard Version Bible, copyright © 1989 by the Division of Christian Education of the National Council of the Churches of Christ in the USA and used by permission.

Cover photograph © The Stock Market/Ariel Skelley, 1996

Cover background art is a detail from *Die Hochzeit zu Kana* by Julius Schnorr von Carolsfeld, Kunsthalle Hamburg, Glockengießerwall, 20095 Hamburg, Germany.

Cover design by Marti Naughton
Text design by Elizabeth Boyce

Library of Congress Cataloging-in-Publication Data

Mackall, Dandi Daley.
    Kindred sisters : New Testament women speak to us today : a book for meditation and reflection / by Dandi Mackall.
    p.   cm.
    Includes bibliographical references and index.
    ISBN 0-8066-2828-6 (alk. paper)
    1. Women in the Bible.   2. Bible. N.T.—Biography.   3. Women—Religious life.   I. Title.
BS2445.M23 1996
225.9'22'082—dc20
                           96-23165
                             CIP

Manufactured in the U.S.A.   AF 9-2828

5   6   7   8   9   10

Contents

Changed Women

Courageous Women

Enterprising Women

Letter from the Author

For a long time I have felt a bond with the women of the New Testament. Although they lived in a different time and different culture, their experiences were not all that different from mine.

The New Testament women in this book were affected by Jesus, who understood and cared about each of them. Jesus taught women; he made them his friends. And he entrusted them with the news of salvation. To transform these women into his chosen disciples, Jesus crossed social, cultural, and gender barriers. And he crosses the same barriers today.

Women are still being transformed by Christ. In return, they are still transforming their families and communities. I have talked with hundreds of such women—kindred sisters—and they are changing the world. Their stories and examples complete the cycle of Christ's transformation.

You may wish to read this book with other women. In each chapter you will hear the stories of both New Testament women and contemporary women. The bonding section at the end of each chapter is for you personally, as are the prayers. But they can be used in group study very effectively, with women sharing their own stories and praying and working together for new or enriched transformations in their own lives.

May God help you form a kinship with the women of the New Testament and apply it to your own role in the world as one of Christ's disciples.

—*Dandi Daley Mackall*

If any of you is lacking in wisdom, ask
God, who gives to all generously and
ungrudgingly, and it will be given you.
(James 1:5)

Wise Women

Elizabeth
Mary
Anna

Lord, thank you for the wise women who loved you such a long time ago. Help me understand them and appreciate their openness to you and to each other. Show me how I can be like them, how your wisdom can be in me, and connect me with others and with my New Testament sisters. Make me wise as I study the wise women, Elizabeth, Mary, and Anna. Amen.

Elizabeth

In the days of King Herod of Judea, there was a priest named Zechariah, who belonged to the priestly order of Abijah. His wife was a descendant of Aaron, and her name was Elizabeth. Both of them were righteous before God, living blamelessly according to all the commandments and regulations of the Lord. But they had no children, because Elizabeth was barren, and both were getting on in years.

Then there appeared to [Zechariah] an angel of the Lord, standing at the right side of the altar of incense. When Zechariah saw him, he was terrified; and fear overwhelmed him. But the angel said to him, "Do not be afraid, Zechariah, for your prayer has been heard. Your wife Elizabeth will bear you a son, and you will name him John."

After those days his wife Elizabeth conceived, and for five months she remained in seclusion. She said, "This is what the Lord has done for me when he looked favorably on me and took away the disgrace I have endured among my people." (Luke 1:5-7, 11-13, 24-25)

When Elizabeth heard Mary's greeting, the child leaped in her womb. And Elizabeth was filled with the Holy Spirit. (Luke 1:41)

1

∞

The Wisdom of Faith

Elizabeth and the Wisdom of Faith

When Luke set out to tell the story of Jesus, he began with Elizabeth and Zechariah, a priestly couple living in the Judean hill country. In those days the Roman Empire dominated the Jewish nation, and Herod ruled as king over Judea. The Jewish religion was kept alive by priests like Zechariah.

Some religious leaders, such as the Pharisees, made a show of keeping the Jewish commandments and regulations concerning purity. Although the Pharisees were revered by most Jewish people, Jesus condemned their hypocrisy. Elizabeth and Zechariah were not like the Pharisees, however. They observed the Lord's commandments in a way that pleased God. *Both of them were righteous before God, living blamelessly according to all the commandments and regulations of the Lord* (Luke 1:6).

Elizabeth held an honorable position in the Jewish community because she had descended from the priestly line of Aaron. And as the wife of a priest, she was considered one of the most important women in Israel.

Elizabeth had everything going for her, except for one sorrow— she had no children. Jewish society considered children wealth and counted sons as old age insurance. Some Jews believed immortality lay in children since only through offspring could they hope to see their name continue. Children were not a choice; they were an inheritance. To be childless was to be cursed by God. Elizabeth was barren and now too old to have children.

Elizabeth and her husband lived outside of Jerusalem, close enough to the temple for Zechariah to carry out his priestly duties. Zechariah served as one of an estimated 20,000 priests in Israel. Since Israel had too many priests to minister daily, they were divided into twenty-four groups. These groups took turns working in the temple, managing its upkeep, teaching God's Word, and directing worship services.

One Sabbath, Zechariah's Abijah division was on duty in Jerusalem. As usual, lots or dice were used to see who would enter the Holy of Holies to burn incense at the altar. The lot fell to Zechariah, giving him a once-in-a-lifetime opportunity.

As the worshippers waited outside, Zechariah entered the inner sanctuary, which was considered God's actual dwelling place. There an angel of the Lord appeared and announced to Zechariah that Elizabeth would bear a son. In the spirit of Elijah, this son would prepare the people for the coming Lord.

"How will I know that this is so?" Zechariah asked the angel Gabriel. *"For I am an old man, and my wife is getting on in years"* (Luke 1:18).

Because of his doubts, Zechariah was struck speechless, but the promise of a child stood. We don't know the details of how Zechariah explained God's promise of a son to Elizabeth. But with the wisdom of faith, Elizabeth believed.

Elizabeth had less information to go on than any of the people who appear in the first Christmas story. Mary, Joseph, and Zechariah all received visits from an angel. Even the shepherds heard an angelic announcement. Not Elizabeth.

Not only did Elizabeth have to get her information second hand from her husband, she must have had to settle for some form of written or impromptu sign language communication from him . Zechariah couldn't use his verbal skills to convince his wife of the angel's promise.

When Elizabeth did understand that God promised to give her a son, she had two choices. She could look at what she could see in front of her—an old man and an old woman physically incapable of conception. Or she could choose to place her faith in the unseen— a promise that after all these years God would make her pregnant.

It couldn't have been an easy choice. What if she failed once again to conceive? Could she face another disappointment? But with no visible, physical evidence to convince her, Elizabeth believed that God would give her a son. And God fulfilled the promise. Elizabeth gave birth to the prophet John the Baptist. Jesus would say of John: *"Truly I tell you, among those born of women no one has arisen greater than John the Baptist"* (Matthew 11:11).

Hebrews 11:1 defines faith as *the assurance of things hoped for, the conviction of things not seen.* Elizabeth was wise in her faith in the unseen promises of God.

Today's Wise Women of Faith

Women today face the same choice Elizabeth had. Will we believe only what we can see, or will our faith extend to God's unseen promises? Like Elizabeth, we need the wisdom of faith.

Trish graduated from college and joined a trainee program for a large corporation. "It's a cut-throat business," Trish explained. "My co-workers lie and steal my customers, and they get rewarded for it. I keep playing straight, but I don't see the rewards. I know there is a reward with God though, even if I can't always see it." Trish has the wisdom of faith in God's unseen rewards.

Lucinda has that same wisdom, but in a much different arena. Lucinda is a young, mentally impaired Christian who understands her struggle with anger as a struggle between the seen and the unseen. "When somebody makes me mad, I know Jesus is there telling me he loves me and I shouldn't let somebody else get me upset. But I can't see Jesus, and I can see the person in front of me making me mad." Lucinda is wise in her faith that the unseen Jesus is always near and promises to help her.

In the same way Lucinda counts on the nearness of Jesus, Amanda has been counting on Jesus to help her through a rough period in her life. In the two years Amanda has been job hunting, she has had her share of disappointments. "So many times I thought I had the job. Then I'd find out I didn't. I had to keep reminding myself to have faith that Christ would help me find a job. It would just be a whole lot easier if I could open an envelope and see Jesus' face instead of another bill!"

2 Corinthians 4:18 says, *We look not at what can be seen but at what cannot be seen; for what can be seen is temporary, but what cannot be seen is eternal.* Placing our faith in God, whom we can't see, is trusting in the eternal. That's true wisdom.

Elizabeth's son grew up to be John the Baptist. Many people heard John and saw Jesus and believed. Yet Jesus praised those who believed in the unseen. When Thomas demanded to see the wounds in Jesus' hands and side before he would believe in the resurrected Christ, Jesus allowed it. But he told Thomas, *"Blessed are those who have not seen and yet have come to believe"* (John 20:29).

Seeing doesn't necessarily lead us to believing. Elizabeth teaches us that believing in the unseen leads to seeing.

Bonding with Our Sister, Elizabeth

Elizabeth was wise in faith. We, too, can practice the wisdom of faith. List ten things you believe without seeing. How do those beliefs show themselves in your actions and relationships with others? How has God blessed you for believing without seeing?

2

❦

The Wisdom of Joy

Elizabeth and the Wisdom of Joy

Elizabeth must have been joyful when she became pregnant after so many childless years. Yet in spite of all she had to be thankful for, Elizabeth might have found some fairly good reasons not to be joyful. She was one of the most important women in Israel, married to a priest, respected by all, blameless before God. Wasn't she the obvious choice for mother of the Messiah? In a national referendum between Mary and Elizabeth, Elizabeth surely would have won easily. Could God have picked any worthier earthly parents than Elizabeth and Zechariah?

Yet God didn't choose Elizabeth. Instead, God chose Elizabeth's unwed, teenage cousin for the job! Mary—not Elizabeth—would receive the honor of becoming the most blessed woman in history. Elizabeth's son would have one purpose in life: to prepare the way for Mary's son. Elizabeth's child would declare himself unworthy to tie the sandal of Mary's son Jesus. Jesus' fame would increase, while John's fame would decrease.

When Elizabeth was faced with the choice between jealousy or joy, she chose joy. In her sixth month, Elizabeth received a visit from her young cousin Mary. When the two pregnant women first saw each other, Elizabeth joyfully exclaimed: *"Blessed are you among women."* She might have added, "And I'm not," but she didn't. Elizabeth

16

opted for unselfish joy over what God was doing through Mary. Elizabeth greeted her cousin, *"And why has this happened to me, that the mother of my Lord comes to me?"* (Luke 1:43).

God had been generous to Elizabeth in giving her a child in her old age. Elizabeth was grateful. That gratitude wasn't lessened when she learned about God's generous gift to Mary. Elizabeth was happy for Mary, too.

Today's Wise Women

Most of us face that same choice over and over—Elizabeth's choice between jealousy or unselfish joy. Three years ago, Marilyn became a member of the growing "sandwich generation," middle-aged people who find themselves spread thin between children who still need their support and parents who also need support. Her mother's Alzheimer's condition made it necessary for Marilyn to bring her mom home to live with her. Marilyn and her husband had worked for twenty-five years, sent two sons to college, yet still couldn't retire. Instead of joining friends for cruises in the summer and warm months in Phoenix in the winter, Marilyn remains tied to home.

Every single day, Marilyn has a choice of attitudes. She can choose jealousy—of other women who aren't part of a generational sandwich. Or, she can choose joy—for blessings that fall to someone else's family.

Marilyn struggles with added responsibilities. Rita, a divorced mom with married children, wrestles with reduced responsibilities. As an empty-nest mother, Rita often misses her grown children. She dines with friends on Christmas Eve, but she remembers those early, happy family Christmases when the kids were little. Rita chooses joy over jealousy. She tries to delight in the happiness of other, younger families, as well as her own.

In very young children there is occasionally a child-like joy that defies grown-up jealousy. It may be related to the child-like faith Christ praised. Whatever it is, it's worth imitating.

One day my daughter Jenny raced home from kindergarten and burst into the house. "Mom! Mom! Guess what!"

"What?" I asked, anticipating great possibilities.

"Alison Sawyer," Jenny continued, catching her breath. "She can tie her own shoe laces all by herself!"

And you can't, came my first thought.

Why could Alison tie her laces while Jenny couldn't? Was my daughter the only child in kindergarten who would have to wear slip-ons the rest of her life? Yet Jenny's joy embraced a wisdom far beyond her years, a wisdom I prayed God would give me, also.

Jesus once told a parable about workers in a vineyard. A group of workers was hired early in the day. The workers labored all day; then each was paid a fair day's wage. When a separate group of workers hired late in the day received the same wage as the all-day workers, the first group complained. The landowner rebuked those complaining workers and said, *"Am I not allowed to do what I choose with what belongs to me? Or are you envious because I am generous?"* (Matthew 20:15).

Every day we look around us and see God's generosity to others. We can choose to react to these blessings with joy or jealousy. If we follow the example of the first wise woman, we'll choose joy. Then like our sister Elizabeth, we will discover more joy—joy over what God gives to us, and unselfish joy over what God gives to others.

Bonding with Our Sister, Elizabeth

Elizabeth was blessed with the wisdom of unselfish joy. Look for something you can be joyful over—a blessing that has been given to someone else. Pray for Elizabeth's gift of unselfish joy. Give thanks for God's goodness to that other person. Tell that person you are happy for her.

3

❧

The Wisdom of the Spirit

Elizabeth and the Wisdom of the Spirit

When Mary came to visit, Elizabeth understood immediately what God was doing through her cousin. Elizabeth showed a depth of spiritual wisdom by becoming the first person to acknowledge Mary as the mother of the Messiah.

When Elizabeth heard Mary's greeting, the child leaped in her womb. And Elizabeth was filled with the Holy Spirit and exclaimed with a loud cry, "Blessed are you among women, and blessed is the fruit of your womb" (Luke 1:41-42).

Filled with the Spirit, Elizabeth had insight and wisdom beyond human understanding. 1 Corinthians talks about two kinds of wisdom—human wisdom and God's wisdom. *We speak of these things in words not taught by human wisdom but taught by the Spirit, interpreting spiritual things to those who are spiritual. Those who are unspiritual do not receive the gifts of God's Spirit, for they are foolishness to them, and they are unable to understand them because they are spiritually discerned. Those who are spiritual discern all things* (1 Corinthians 2:13-15).

Elizabeth was spiritual, and that spirituality enabled her to discern what was happening around her. First, she understood what God was doing for her. In the middle of God's vast plan for the entire human race, Elizabeth saw John as God's personal gift to her. *"This is what the Lord has done for me when he looked favorably on me and took away the disgrace I have endured among my people"* (Luke 1:25).

Next, Elizabeth understood how God was working in Mary. She discerned that Mary was pregnant with the Chosen Son. Because Elizabeth had the wisdom of the Spirit, she knew how to help Mary. Her insight must have encouraged and reaffirmed Mary's own faith, because Mary responded in an outpouring of praise.

Elizabeth was filled with the Spirit. The fruit of that Spirit poured from her as she showed *love* for God in return for God's blessing to her. She manifested *joy* for Mary over God's promise of a Son, *peace* with her own role in God's work, *patience* in waiting, *kindness* and *generosity* to her cousin Mary, and *humility* in praise.

Today's Wise Women

Today we need God's spiritual wisdom as much as women did in Elizabeth's day. As we experience the wisdom of God's Spirit, we discern how God is working in the world. We can be encouraged, and we can encourage others as Elizabeth encouraged Mary.

Gail is in her early twenties. She has several job opportunities that could affect the rest of her life. She says, "I can see two brands of wisdom when I try to make decisions. Most people advise me to go where the most money is. But when I listen to God, when I pray and read the Bible, I can see other factors, too. Where will I be less distracted? Can I keep other commitments? Where will I grow more as a person? Sometimes the two wisdoms add up to the same decision, and sometimes they don't." Gail prays for God's wisdom. Recently she turned down a top job offer because she didn't feel God wanted her to move.

Last year was the first Christmas Bev and her children faced since the death of Bev's husband. She explained the kind of wisdom God gave her to help her family get through the holidays: "Every morning I asked God to fill me with the Spirit of Wisdom. Sometimes I looked at my kids and had no idea what they needed. Then I'd get this insight, an understanding. Christy needed to be alone that day. Jason should have a night out with me. Karen should spend some time with my sister's family. It was God's Spirit giving me that wisdom."

Carolyn had another reason for seeking God's wisdom. "I'm fairly settled and content with my life," she explained. "But I need spiritual wisdom so I don't miss what's going on around me. There's so much I do miss if I'm not filled with God. I forget to look for ways I can help people. I might not notice that my mother has needs she didn't have before. I need a spiritual sensitivity or I go stale!"

Anita said her life verse was Ephesians 5:18: *Do not get drunk with wine, for that is debauchery; but be filled with the Spirit.* "I know what it means to be drunk with wine because I was a practicing alcoholic for eleven years," she said. "Alcohol controlled everything I thought and did, how I talked and walked. Now I try to let God's Spirit fill me that completely. I want God's thoughts to be mine. I want every action to be not just affected, but controlled by the Spirit."

The apostle Paul wrote, *We have not ceased praying for you and asking that you may be filled with the knowledge of God's will in all spiritual wisdom and understanding* (Colossians 1:9). Elizabeth understood what God was doing because God filled her with the Spirit. We can ask God for that same wisdom of Spirit.

Bonding with Our Sister, Elizabeth

Elizabeth was wise in Spirit. That wisdom allowed her to minister to Mary and understand how God was working in their lives. Pray that God will fill you with the Spirit of Wisdom. Ask the Holy Spirit to use you this week to encourage or help someone else. Then on the phone, in a letter, or face to face, encourage or help that person. Later, record what happened when you did. What can you do next?

A Prayer for Elizabeth's Wisdom

Lord, thank you for the example of wisdom I see in my sister Eliza-beth. Help me to identify with her. Teach me to trust even when I don't see. Help me to be joyful for the blessings others receive, as well as for those that come to me. As you filled Elizabeth with the Spirit, fill me with your Spirit of Wisdom. Amen

$\mathcal{M}$ary

In the sixth month the angel Gabriel was sent by God to a town in Galilee called Nazareth, to a virgin engaged to a man whose name was Joseph, of the house of David. The virgin's name was Mary. And he came to her and said, "Greetings, favored one! The Lord is with you." But she was much perplexed by his words and pondered what sort of greeting this might be. The angel said to her, "Do not be afraid, Mary, for you have found favor with God. And now, you will conceive in your womb and bear a son, and you will name him Jesus. . . . He will reign over the house of Jacob forever, and of his kingdom there will be no end." Mary said to the angel, "How can this be, since I am a virgin?" The angel said to her, "The Holy Spirit will come upon you, and the power of the Most High will overshadow you; therefore the child to be born will be holy; he will be called Son of God." Then Mary said, "Here am I, the servant of the Lord; let it be with me according to your word." Then the angel departed from her. (Luke 1:26-31, 33-35, 38)

And she gave birth to her firstborn son and wrapped him in bands of cloth, and laid him in a manger, because there was no place for them in the inn. (Luke 2:7)

4

∞

The Wisdom of Humility

Mary and the Wisdom of Humility

Mary lived in Nazareth, a little-known village in Galilee filled with farmers and artisans. Rome had controlled Nazareth and all of Palestine for half a century. Most Jews believed a messiah would come and deliver them from their oppressors. Although generally unschooled, many young girls like Mary may have dreamed of being the chosen virgin of Isaiah 7:14 who would *bear a son, and . . . name him Immanuel.*

When a girl reached the age of twelve years and a day, she was eligible for betrothal. The average age of a man at the time of his betrothal was sixteen to twenty-two years. It's unlikely that Mary would have been older than thirteen when she became betrothed to Joseph.

In many ways betrothal resembled our modern idea of marriage more than what we think of today as engagement. Sometimes an elaborate betrothal ceremony took the place of a traditional wedding. Joseph would have paid his prospective father-in-law a sum of money for his new bride. Mary's consent to the union was probably required. For all practical purposes, after the betrothal she would become the property of her husband.

Legally the betrothed were considered husband and wife. If Joseph died before consummating his marriage, the community would consider Mary a widow in every respect. Once married, only a husband could get a legal divorce, and he could get it any time he tired of his wife. As a Jewish woman, Mary's circumstances were humble, but now she was about to become the most exalted woman in history.

During these days of Mary's betrothal, the angel Gabriel made his announcement to Mary in Nazareth. *"You will conceive in your womb, and bear a son, and you will name him Jesus."*

"How can this be," Mary asked the angel, *"since I am a virgin?"*

Gabriel answered, *"The Holy Spirit will come upon you, and the power of the Most High will overshadow you; therefore the child to be born will be holy; he will be called the Son of God"* (Luke 1:31-35).

What a test of true humility! In a matter of a few minutes Mary learned she would become pregnant by the Holy Spirit and give birth to God's Son! Mary's response shows the balance inherent in wise humility. *"Here am I, the servant of the Lord; let it be with me according to your word"* (Luke 1:38). Mary didn't think so highly of herself that she felt she deserved the honor. Neither did she think so lowly of herself that she refused the honor God was giving her.

Humility can be defined as thinking wisely about ourselves—not overestimating our position and abilities but not underestimating ourselves either. Paul wrote to the Romans, *For by the grace given to me I say to everyone among you not to think of yourself more highly than you ought to think, but to think with sober judgment* (Romans 12:3).

If we are wise in humility, we won't think so highly of ourselves that we fail to serve others. Jesus humbled himself while he was on earth. *"Take my yoke upon you, and learn from me; for I am gentle and humble in heart, and you will find rest for your souls"* (Matthew 11:29). This kind of humbling isn't a feeling of unworthiness but a wise choice to learn and to serve.

In fact, most of the biblical verses about humility are about serving others. The Old Testament prophet Micah wrote, *And what does the* LORD *require of you but to do justice, and to love kindness, and to walk humbly with your God?* (Micah 6:8). If we think too highly of ourselves, we won't stoop to help other people. Mary was ready to be considered a servant so that she could be used by God.

Philippians says, *Do nothing from selfish ambition or conceit, but in humility regard others as better than yourselves* (2:3). Being told to regard others as better than ourselves does not mean we should deny our self worth and believe others are worth more than we are. The next verse explains. *Let each of you look not to your own interests, but to the interests of others* (2:4). Without denying any of our worth to God, we choose to *act* in humility. We want to help other people, as if they were worth a fortune! Mary was given the highest honor granted to a woman—to become the mother of God's Son. Yet she realized her blessing was given so that she could serve.

Humility also means not holding a low opinion of ourselves. Wise humility has nothing to do with low self-esteem. We aren't called to believe we're worthless. Christ died for us! Colossians warns believers away from a false humility of self-abasement. *Do not let anyone disqualify you, insisting on self-abasement. . . . These have indeed an appearance of wisdom in promoting self-imposed piety, humility, and severe treatment of the body, but they are of no value in checking self-indulgence* (Colossians 2:18-23). Feeling sorry for ourselves or complaining about our inadequacies is not humility. When Jesus left heaven to be born and die on earth, he *humbled* himself. He wasn't worth less; he was still fully God. He chose humility to become like us and to serve.

The apostle Paul showed the same kind of wise humility as Mary when he wrote, *But by the grace of God I am what I am* (I Corinthians 15:10). Mary said, *"My soul magnifies the Lord, and my spirit rejoices in God my Savior, for he has looked with favor on the lowliness of his servant. Surely, from now on all generations will call me blessed"* (Luke 1:46-48).

Mary might have complained that she was too young to be a mother, much less the mother of God's Son. She was poor and lacked knowledge of the world beyond Nazareth. Yet in humble wisdom, Mary accepted the tremendous task God had for her.

Today's Wise Women of Humility

God still calls us to do great things. We need to respond like Mary, with wise humility that leads to serving others. Julie's novels and short stories have won many awards, but she still takes time to help new writers develop their skills. She knows her talent better than anyone else, but she maintains humility. She says, "Never listen to your own press! I'm the same person whether I write a book everybody loves or a flop. I don't believe I'm on this earth to help only myself, so I try to help other writers whenever I can." Julie doesn't deny the praise others give her work, but she offers her talent to serve.

Ney is another woman who might be tempted away from the wisdom of humility. As a young Christian counselor, Ney is respected by many women who feel they owe her their lives or their sanity. Ney recognizes the dangers of unnecessarily inflating or deflating her counseling abilities. Some days, she admits, she feels she has all the answers to life's problems. Other days she feels as if she can't be trusted to run her own life. Every day she tries to accept herself and not overestimate or underestimate her skills so that she can better serve her patients.

When my daughter was four, she taught me a lesson in wise humility. Jenny tried to cut out hearts for Valentine's Day. When she brought me her odd-shaped pieces of paper, I assumed the role of cheerleader. "Jenny," I exclaimed in a falsetto. "These are so great!" But Jenny wisely evaluated her own work, separating the paper pieces into two piles. "No, Mom," she said. She pointed to the first pile, containing true heart shapes. "These ones are great." Pointing to the other pile, she announced, "These ones are not." She was comfortable with an accurate picture of her work—not too high, not too low.

Proverbs 15:33 says, *The fear of the* LORD *is instruction in wisdom, and humility goes before honor.* Mary was wise in her humility, and God honored her.

Bonding with Our Sister, Mary

Like Mary, we need to be wise in humility so that we can be free to consider the needs of others. Choose one person whose needs you will consider more important than your own this week. Write at least five actions you can carry out humbly for this person. (Go shopping with her, even though you hate shopping; suggest an activity he [or she] loves, even though you don't love it; write or call even when it's not convenient for you; visit; etc.)

5

∞

The Wisdom of Flexibility

Mary and the Wisdom of Flexibility

Mary, the youngest of the wise women we'll discuss, probably planned to marry the carpenter Joseph and live happily ever after in Nazareth. She didn't plan to be an unwed, pregnant teenager.

Following the startling announcement that she would bear God's only Son, Mary traveled to see her older cousin Elizabeth. Elizabeth lived in the hill country outside of Jerusalem. Although people seldom ventured farther than a day's journey, Mary's journey through rugged terrain on foot or on a donkey would have taken several days to a week.

We don't know what Mary expected when she returned home to Nazareth. Would her family know she was pregnant? Would God tell each of *them* in a dream? Would Joseph be waiting for her? Or maybe what waited for her would be stoning or ostracism.

Soon Mary was discovered to be pregnant, and Joseph decided to divorce her privately. She may have started packing for her exile. Then the angel Gabriel paid another visit, this time to Joseph in a dream. Gabriel explained that Mary was pregnant by the Holy Spirit. Joseph should not be afraid to take her as his wife. They married quietly, without the wedding celebration Mary may have hoped for.

Mary surely would have preferred a comfortable place to have her baby, but that was not to be. Near the end of Mary's pregnancy,

Caesar Augustus decreed a worldwide census. Because Joseph descended from David's line, he was required to be counted at Bethlehem, "the City of David" (Matthew 2:4). Mary accompanied her husband on the ninety-mile journey.

While Mary and Joseph were in Bethlehem, the time came for Mary to give birth. Mary probably hadn't expected to deliver her baby in a stable, but no other room was available. Stables were generally nothing more than caves near inns.

After the birth of Jesus, Mary and Joseph expected to stay in Bethlehem. Again, their plans changed. Joseph was warned in a dream to flee to Egypt because King Herod wanted to kill the new king, Jesus. So Mary and Joseph went to Egypt and remained there until King Herod died. The couple then intended to return to Judea, but God led them to Nazareth instead.

How Mary handled all those changes reveals one of the secrets of her wisdom. Mary knew what it meant to be flexible. *"How can this be, since I am a virgin?"* This was Mary's perfectly natural response to Gabriel's message. She had probably dreamt about her new life with Joseph. She had a wedding to plan. Now all that was over. How could this be? It wasn't what she had expected. A baby didn't fit into her plans—not so soon.

God knows we're human. It's okay to ask, "How can this be?" Mary asked, and Gabriel didn't criticize her for asking. We can echo Mary's question when we are hit with the unexpected.

No one has ever been delivered a more important change than Mary. Yet she flexed. She bent toward God and let God's will happen to her. Mary ended her conversation with Gabriel by saying, *"Let it be with me according to your word"* (Luke 1:38). If we can understand Mary's transition from "How can it be?" to "Let it be," maybe we can learn how to be flexible enough to receive God's gifts.

When Mary asked how she could be pregnant and yet still be a virgin, Gabriel told her that the Holy Spirit would come upon her. The angel didn't give an elaborate, scientific explanation about what was to happen. Instead, Mary got a promise: *"For nothing will be impossible with God"* (Luke 1:37).

If God wished, God could make the world and the entire cosmos conform to all *our* plans. God is able to fulfill *our* will. God could easily have fulfilled Mary's modest dream of a conventional family, but God had greater plans. Mary was to be the mother of God's Son!

If God changes our plans, God has better ones. We might not understand. We may need to ask, "How can this be?" But we can still let it be because we know nothing will be impossible with God.

Mary didn't know the details, but she knew God. Right before her acceptance speech, Mary revealed her heart. *"Here am I, the servant of the Lord"* (Luke 1:38). It is because Mary was God's servant that she could come to this point of flexibility, of letting it be. If she had been her own servant, she might have fought harder for *her* plans, *her* wedding, *her* reputation. When our plans don't work out, we also may not understand why. Yet we can imitate Mary's wise flexibility and let it be.

Today's Wise Women of Flexibility

How do we handle situations when things don't go according to our plans? Most of us don't flex naturally. If we have organized ourselves well enough to get everything done, we tell ourselves that the least other people can do is try to fit in.

Kristen found that her inflexibility was leading to depression. After a long relationship, Kristen and her boyfriend broke up. Kristen said, "I woke up each day and expected things to go just as I planned—everyone would love me at work; I'd get everything done; Eric would call and want to get back together. When things didn't work out as I'd planned, I'd get more depressed." Wisely, Kristen learned how to flex. "Every morning I began by reminding myself that no day ever goes entirely according to the best-laid plans. I had to remember that God has plans too. Whatever God had in store for me would be better than my plans."

Like Kristen, Marge had to learn to be flexible. Recently Marge moved into a nursing home. She never expected it to happen to her.

She said, "I've met a lot of wonderful people here that I never would have seen if I'd stayed in my home. When I'm too old to change, it will be time to die. You never know what's around that next corner, and that's life."

Noelle, a college student, realizes her need for the wisdom to bend, to accept what she can't change. She explained, "It all started when my parents divorced. Their separation made it hard for me to be happy. They say they've changed and can't live together. So I guess I have to change so I can live with them apart." Noelle is learning the wisdom of flexibility.

If the only thing that really counts is serving Christ, then like Mary we can accept whatever changes God allows. Nothing will be impossible with God.

Bonding with Our Sister, Mary

Mary was wise and flexible. What plans and expectations do you have this week that may fall through, or may have fallen through already? List positive steps you can take to accept the change and let it be.

6

❧

The Wisdom of Pondering

Mary and the Wisdom of Pondering

Elizabeth and Anna, the other two wise women, had the wisdom of years and experience. Mary didn't have their experience. At a young age, she became the wife of a carpenter and the mother of Jesus. Beyond that, we don't get much of a picture of her life in the outside world. Yet Scripture indicates that a world went on *inside* young Mary. Mary was a ponderer, a deep thinker.

When Gabriel came to Mary with his greeting, Mary pondered the meaning of his words. When the shepherds came to worship the baby Jesus, all who heard them expressed astonishment. *But Mary treasured all these words and pondered them in her heart* (Luke 2:19).

Years later, Mary and Joseph discovered their twelve-year-old son in the temple answering the profound questions of the teachers. Mary and Joseph returned home with Jesus. And Mary *treasured all these things in her heart* (Luke 2:51).

The New Testament Greek word for *ponder* carries the idea of "conferring with oneself." Pondering is similar to meditating; it means to think prayerfully, to mull over.

When Mary learned that she was the one chosen to be the most blessed of women, what did she do? She didn't run and tell everyone about her honor. Instead she went to visit her cousin Elizabeth. Then, instead of immediately sharing her news, she waited for Elizabeth to acknowledge her as the future mother of God's Son.

Mary spent three months with Elizabeth, ninety days to ponder what was happening inside her. She didn't try to fix the world around her—straighten Joseph out, convince him of her innocence, her honor. After Mary returned to Nazareth, wild accusations must have begun flying all around her.

Most of us would have tried to justify ourselves to the outside world. We'd want to convince our family, fiancé, friends, and enemies of our innocence. But Mary's thoughts appear to have been on God, not on herself. She pondered God's acceptance of her. God's Son was inside her. Mary held her peace, and God sent an angel to justify her to Joseph.

Mary remembered the words of Gabriel and the words of the shepherds. She called up those words and pondered them. Remembering is a part of pondering. There is a rich biblical tradition of remembering. God knows our propensity to forget and has given us memory aids. In Old Testament days some people wore Scripture in holders called phylacteries. These hollow cubes held passages from Exodus and Deuteronomy. Phylacteries were worn on the hand, arm, or forehead to remind the Israelites of God's promises. After forty years in the wilderness, the Israelites built altars of stones taken from the flooded Jordan River. The piles of stones reminded them how God had brought them safely out of the wilderness and across the river.

In the New Testament, Jesus instituted communion: *"Do this in remembrance of me"* (Luke 22:19). When we follow this command, we ponder what Jesus has sacrificed for us.

Today's Pondering Women

Our fast-paced society breeds few ponderers. Days filled with school, jobs, family, friends, TV, errands, and other activities leave most of us with little quiet time to think. We need to make our own opportunities to ponder.

Tammy is a college freshman who recognizes the need to be a ponderer like Mary. She said, "I'll go nuts if I don't take breaks from school. I need time to think. Before my morning class on Monday,

Wednesday, and Friday, I sneak off to an empty classroom. It's the only time I can piece together what God's doing in my life." Tammy has learned that she has to plan her quiet, thinking times. They don't just happen.

Latricia has come up with her own aid for pondering. "I can go a whole day without thinking about God unless I set up "triggers" for myself. For example, I got a page-a-day calendar so that every morning when I tear it off, I get myself in the habit of stopping to think about God. Tearing that date off is already a habit. I just use the habit to remind myself to think about what God's doing in my life."

Another idea for pondering comes from a woman whose government job requires an erratic schedule. Di keeps a journal of moments, times when she sees glimpses of God's work on earth. She began this practice the day she broke up with her boyfriend and realized how many thoughts she had given to him. She wanted her mind to be filled with Christ as it had been filled with her boyfriend. Di also writes down "word photos" to ponder things she sees as God's handiwork—trees encased with ice, a child reaching for her mother.

Mary had a lot to ponder. What did she think about as the body of Jesus formed and grew inside her? If we have come to a belief in Christ, then through the Spirit, Christ has come to live in us. We have a lot to ponder, too.

I have been crucified with Christ; and it is no longer I who live, but it is Christ who lives in me (Galatians 2:19-20).

Bonding with Our Sister, Mary

Mary had the wisdom to ponder the work of God. Let us be wise in our own thoughts of God's work in us. Make a list of things God has done or is doing in your life. Take time out today to ponder. Meditate on what it means to have Christ living inside you. Participate in communion and whatever services your church offers to help you remember Christ.

A Prayer for Mary's Wisdom

Lord, thank you for the example of my sister Mary. Help me identify with her gentle and humble spirit. Cause me to see myself as you see me and accept myself as you accept me. Forgive me when I fail to let go of my own plans. I want to be open to receive your plans for me. Keep my mind focused on you. Teach me to remember all you've done for me and all I can learn from Mary. Amen

$\mathcal{A}$nna

There was also a prophet, Anna the daughter of Phanuel, of the tribe of Asher. She was of a great age, having lived with her husband seven years after her marriage, then as a widow to the age of eighty-four. She never left the temple but worshiped there with fasting and prayer night and day. At that moment she came, and began to praise God and to speak about the child to all who were looking for the redemption of Jerusalem. (Luke 2:36-38)

7

∞

The Wisdom of Waiting

Anna and the Wisdom of Waiting

In the Hebrew world at the time of Christ, it was said that the only truly "free" woman was a widow. If that's true, then our third wise woman was the most liberated of the three—even though for years she had scarcely left the temple in Jerusalem.

Anna was waiting and worshiping in the temple the day Joseph and Mary walked in with baby Jesus.

Mary and Joseph planned to stay in Bethlehem long enough to observe all the ceremonies required by Jewish law. On the eighth day after his birth, Jesus had been circumcised and officially named. It was also tradition for a firstborn son to be presented to God after birth. This ceremony involved a "redeeming," or a buying back of the child from God through an offering.

For forty days after Jesus' birth, Mary was considered ceremonially unclean, and she could not enter the temple. At the end of this period of separation, she and Joseph were required by law to bring a lamb for a burnt offering and a turtle dove for a sin offering. If they could not afford a lamb, they were allowed to bring two doves instead. This is what Mary and Joseph did.

It was during this visit to the temple to dedicate their son and fulfill the laws of purification that Mary and Joseph met the third wise woman we'll discuss. Anna, whose name means "gracious," was there waiting.

Anna was a daughter of Phanuel from the Israelite tribe of Asher. Asher was one of the dispersed, or scattered, tribes that were considered insignificant. In her youth, Anna had been married for seven years. Then her husband died. Anna never remarried.

Luke records that Anna was a widow of eighty-four years. It is unclear whether she had been widowed eighty-four years, making her age over one hundred, or whether she was eighty-four years old when Mary brought Jesus to the temple. Anna may have lodged in the women's courts of the temple or in an adjoining alms-house or apartment. She was a prophetess, and she stayed in or near the temple to be available for those who wanted to consult her. As a prophetess, Anna was esteemed as knowing the mind of God.

Anna walked in at the precise instant when the Christ Child was presented in the temple. There before her was the redemption of Israel. For Anna, now at least eighty-four years old, it had been a long wait.

God's perfect will involves perfect timing. In the fullness of time, God brought forth a Son. Jesus on earth was conscious of his Father's perfect timing. All through the Gospel of John, Jesus explains his actions with, *"My time has not yet come."* Finally, just before his arrest in the garden, he says, *"The hour has come"* (John 17:1).

God had promised that the redemption of Israel would come in the form of the Messiah. From Anna's perspective, she had waited a lifetime to see that promise fulfilled. From God's perspective, that wait was only a moment in time.

We experience the difference in time perspectives when we work with children. Have you ever made a young child wait for your help? "I need you!" he might say. You holler back, "I'm coming." You know you are on your way; you just have to finish what you were doing first. You might be gathering all you need to help him. You *are* coming soon. But to the waiting child, it seems like forever. In the same way, when God promises to come, that promise will be fulfilled. No matter how long the wait, the timing will be perfect.

God's perfect timing ensures that we end up with the best gift. Genesis 2 tells us that God created Adam but didn't follow directly with Eve. Instead, Adam was assigned the task of naming the animals. Adam may have felt ready for a companion who resembled him more closely than the giraffe or the duck. But there he sat, tossing out animal names as they all filed by: "Bear, monkey, elephant."

By the time God got around to making Eve, Adam was ready. When he saw the woman God had created, he might have declared, "Wow! This is more like it—bone of my bone and flesh of my flesh!" Eve was worth the wait.

Today's Wise Women

Our world spins too fast for us to wait in a supermarket line. We have fast food, fast lanes, drive-thrus, and quick stops. We resent being kept waiting for even a few minutes.

Anna, our third wise woman, waited a lifetime. We can remember her wait and her reward, the fulfillment of God's promise in the Christ child. Then we too can wait as long as God calls us to wait.

Dorothea waited a long time for the answer to her prayer. But her husband ridiculed her faith. "I prayed for him every day for over forty-seven years. When God answered that prayer and my husband accepted Jesus, I said I could die happy. Instead, God has given us the best eight years of our lives together!" Dorothea, like Anna, knows the wisdom of waiting.

Marlene is still waiting for God to answer her prayer. Marlene's parents emigrated from China before her birth. Even though Marlene has never visited China, she prays regularly that more Chinese people would find Christ and be able to worship him publicly. When I asked her how she would feel if she never saw her prayers for China answered, Marlene said, "I will pray for them and do all I can until I die. And then I will wait longer to see the answer from heaven." Marlene is wise in her waiting.

Sara is a college student who admits she has learned what she knows about waiting from her grandmother. "Every time I start to complain about things not going my way—like no boyfriend, no summer job—Gram gets this patient smile on her face. She tells me about her grandparents who were slaves. She says they did all they could and waited for what they couldn't do. Then she tells me to do the same."

When God makes us wait, we can remember Anna's lifetime of waiting. Just as seeing the promised Christ child was worth the wait for Anna; seeing God's promises will be worth our wait, too.

Bonding with Our Sister, Anna

Our older sister Anna was wise in waiting. Think of two things you have had to wait for in your life. How long did you wait for each? Were they worth the wait? Now write down two promises of God you should be waiting for. (Be specific: salvation for someone you love, freedom from spousal abuse, peace concerning your children's decisions, acceptance or forgiveness of one who's wronged you, justice for the poor.) What will you pray, and what will you do while you wait?

8

The Wisdom of Hope

Anna and the Wisdom of Hope

Anna was a prophetess. Although the spirit of prophecy in Israel had ceased for well over three hundred years, God chose Anna as a prophet. God gave this woman the important job of prophesying the arrival of the Christ child. Anna had been faithful and wise in hope, and now she saw her hope fulfilled in Jesus.

Anna comes from a long line of biblical prophetesses. In the New Testament, the word "prophetess" means someone who speaks forth or speaks openly. A prophet or prophetess was a proclaimer of a divine message rather than a fortune teller of the future.

God or special messengers of God had appeared to women before Anna: Eve, Hagar, Sarah, the mother of Samson. Miriam is the first prophetess named in the Bible. She led the children of Israel in their song of triumph at the Red Sea. Deborah served God both as a prophetess and as a judge. Isaiah found an unnamed prophetess and took her as his wife. King Josiah needed the wisdom of the prophetess Huldah to interpret the word of the Lord when the book of the law (Deuteronomy) was discovered.

The widow Anna followed these godly women in the office of prophetess. Anna spent her life in prayer and service. In her wisdom, she hoped to fulfill God's purpose for her. When the time came for her hope to be realized, Anna was ready.

Although we may only be concerned about what's at the end of a waiting period, God cares about the process of waiting itself. Waiting can change us. Anna surely grew in spirituality during those years of waiting in the temple. I wish we had more details about Anna's life, a before-and-after sketch of the prophetess. Waiting for perhaps sixty years, fasting, praying, and serving must have had a profound effect on Anna's character. Even in the midst of the grand scheme for all people, God cared about the process of Anna's spiritual growth.

The years Anna waited in the temple prepared and refined her as a prophetess. Forty years earlier, she may not have recognized that the baby Mary and Joseph brought into the temple was the Messiah. Jesus said, *"Blessed are the pure in heart, for they will see God"* (Matthew 5:8). Anna's years in the temple purified her so that she could see God. If God makes us wait, we can interpret our waiting period as a process that will help prepare us for a gift.

Sometimes even God's most faithful servants don't always see their hopes realized. They may wait their whole lives and never receive the answer to their prayers. But they are still wise in hope if they place their trust in God.

Hebrews 11 is sometimes called the "Hall of Faith." In this chapter are listed prophets and heroes who accomplished great feats because of their faith in God. By faith, Sarah, biologically too old to bear children, received the ability to conceive. By faith, Rahab, the prostitute in Jericho, did not perish with the disobedient because she had received the Hebrew spies in peace (Hebrews 11.35).

But there are others listed in the same Hall of Faith—people who were stoned to death, persecuted, tormented. These people had the faith of heroes like Sarah, Miriam, and Rahab. Yet they didn't receive what they had hoped for. *Yet all these, though they were commended for their faith, did not receive what was promised* (Hebrews 11:39).

If we are wise in hope, how do we keep from being utterly disappointed when we don't see our hopes realized? By hoping and waiting for the Messiah, Anna risked disappointment. No one likes to be disappointed. Our instincts tell us to protect ourselves from hoping. If we don't expect anything, we won't be disappointed. Yet God calls us to hope, to believe.

Romans 5:5 explains to us the way to hope without disappointment: *And hope does not disappoint us, because God's love has been poured into our hearts through the Holy Spirit that has been given to us.*

We have the promise that hope will not disappoint. Why? Not because we'll always get what we want but because God pours out love in us through the Holy Spirit.

Today's Wise Women of Hope

Anna had the wisdom of hope, the same hope we need today. Sharon's son, when he was young, accepted Christ. When he became a teen, he ran into trouble, joined a street gang, and abused alcohol. Sharon did all she could. She prayed and hoped. "I kept my hope in Jesus," she explained. "I knew my son would come back." Her son did eventually come back to an honest and happy life—but it took twelve years of waiting. Sharon confesses there were times when she got discouraged. But she says, "When my son discouraged me, I looked past him to Jesus. Jesus never disappoints."

Other mothers have experienced the grief of losing a child to drugs, even though they have prayed just as faithfully as Sharon. Like the women in Hebrews 11 who didn't receive what they prayed for, they are still wise in hope. Sometimes all we can do is trust, and that is enough.

Danielle attributes valuable changes in herself to the years she had to wait for a child. After nine years she and her husband adopted two special needs children. Danielle explained, "I'm a better mom than I would have been nine years ago. And look at these kids! They were worth the wait." Like Sharon, Danielle grew wise in hope.

Sabrina went through a long struggle with hope and disappointment. Her dream was to be a great artist. Instead, she taught art to elementary children in her local school. She explained, "I was bitterly disappointed until I realized the best part of my hope *has* been realized. I didn't get the fame, but I got the talent and the chance to develop it and pass it along." Sabrina moved from bitterness to understanding by wisely trusting God's Spirit in her.

Just as Anna was wise in her hope that she would see the Messiah, we can be wise in our hope. God promises that hope will not disappoint us, even though it may not always bring exactly what we hoped for.

Bonding with Our Sister, Anna

Anna showed wisdom in her hope. We can bond with our sister Anna when we find ourselves in God's waiting room. Think of a waiting period in your life—now or in the past. What has the waiting process done for you? On a sheet of paper, make two columns for your answers: 1) Changes in Me; and 2) Disappointments. Thank God for each change, and ask God for the Spirit of Comfort to help you through each disappointment.

9

The Wisdom of Endurance

Anna and the Wisdom of Endurance

Year after year Anna served God in the temple. After so many years of meeting other people's needs, she might have felt she'd earned the right to rest. Wasn't it finally time to take care of herself, to hang a "Please Do Not Disturb" sign on her door? But Anna continued serving in the temple. She endured.

Enduring is not the same as waiting. We know Anna waited for the Christ child, but she also endured. She waited actively without interrupting her service. Endurance is strong, active, and effective waiting.

Anna didn't just sit around the temple until Mary and Joseph walked in with Jesus. She fasted and prayed and actively served God, passing along the message of God's will. *She never left the temple but worshiped there with fasting and prayer night and day* (Luke 2:37).

When the moment finally arrived and Jesus was right in front of her, Anna rejoiced to see the promised Messiah. Here was the gift she had awaited all those years! Yet Anna did not keep the gift for herself. Anna turned directly to the crowds to explain *their* redemption. She seized her chance to tell them about the Christ child. *At that moment she came, and began to praise God and to speak about the child to all who were looking for the redemption of Jerusalem* (Luke 2:38).

Today's Wise Women

If anyone deserves rest, it's Anna and people like her who have spent their lives serving. Art Linkletter wrote a book with a great title, *Old Age Is Not for Sissies*. Some of us may complain about a pulled muscle or tennis elbow, and those conditions do hurt. Yet many older people wake up with pain in nearly every joint. Arthritis is common among the elderly, but that doesn't lessen the constant and acute pain it inflicts. A certain amount of endurance is required for old age.

Rachel lives in poverty in Chicago where she raises seven great-grandchildren. Each day Rachel shows up at government offices within walking distance to see if they can use her to interpret for other Mexican-Americans. She comes home tired but never weary of doing good. "Jesus is my friend," she says, grinning. "He helps me every day, and I look every day to see how I can help my Jesus."

Rachel shares a secret of endurance with the writer of Hebrews who encouraged believers to run the race set before them by *looking to Jesus . . . who for the sake of the joy that was set before him endured the cross* (Hebrews 12:2). Rachel looks to Jesus' example of endurance. By sharing in that struggle, she shares in his joy—and in Anna's. Wise endurance leads to joy. James wrote, *Indeed we call blessed [happy] those who showed endurance* (5:11).

Another elderly believer has experienced the rewards of endurance. Mae went back to school when she turned sixty. She got her degree in teaching and has found fulfillment as a substitute in an inner city school district. She said, "When we feel like marking time with the rest of our lives, God calls us to mark life with the rest of our time."

Naomi has served in her home church in nearly every volunteer position over the last forty years: teacher, janitor, secretary, deacon, committee member, and chairwoman. Naomi's philosophy is that there is always something to do in God's kingdom. She believes the older she gets, the better she should be able to serve.

God gives a promise in Psalm 92:14-15. *In old age they still produce fruit; they are always green and full of sap, showing that the* LORD *is upright.*

Anna's wise endurance shows that God is upright! Our endurance will do the same.

Bonding with Our Sister, Anna

Anna possessed the wisdom of endurance. And she shared that wisdom. Even after she received what she wanted, Anna turned to others. She saw the Christ child, then turned to the crowd to talk about what the child meant to them. Think of one person you can talk to about Christ or one loving act you can do for someone this week. You may think you are too busy or tired to follow through, but you can endure as Anna did. What you share will bring another sister and you greater joy!

A Prayer for Anna's Wisdom

Lord, thank you for the example of Anna the Prophetess. Make me like Anna, strong in faith. Make me pure in heart so that I can recognize you in my world. Help me not to give up. Teach me how to wait on you and hope in you. Thank you for your Spirit that will never disappoint me. Amen.

A Prayer to Follow the Wise Women

Dear Jesus, help me to know you intimately as Elizabeth, Mary, and Anna knew you. Give me the wisdom to accept myself and to continue in hope. Help me take time to ponder and see you at work in the world. Give me the wisdom to turn to others and help them endure and hope. Thank you that no matter how young or old I am, I am always the perfect age to serve you. Remind me of the rich heritage I have in these three wise women. Make me a wise woman, too. Amen

So if anyone is in Christ, there is a new
creation: everything old has passed
away; see, everything has become new!
(2 Corinthians 5:17)

Changed Women

The Woman at the Well
Mary of Bethany
The Hemorrhaging Woman

Lord, thank you for your love that accepts me completely. Thank you for your power that can change me. Help me understand these three women who allowed you to change them—the Samaritan woman at the well, Mary of Bethany, and the hemorrhaging woman. Give me insight to discern how you used these women to change the world. Show me how I can be like my sisters in Christ. Touch me as you touched them. Change me to make me more like Christ. Amen.

The Woman at the Well

A Samaritan woman came to draw water, and Jesus said to her, "Give me a drink." (His disciples had gone to the city to buy food.) The Samaritan woman said to him, "How is it that you, a Jew, ask a drink of me, a woman of Samaria?" (Jews do not share things in common with Samaritans.) Jesus answered her, "If you knew the gift of God, and who it is that is saying to you, 'Give me a drink,' you would have asked him, and he would have given you living water" (John 4:7-10).

The woman said to him, "I know that Messiah is coming" (who is called Christ). "When he comes, he will proclaim all things to us." Jesus said to her, "I am he, the one who is speaking to you." (John 4:25-26)

Many Samaritans from that city believed in him because of the woman's testimony, "He told me everything I have ever done." (John 4:39)

10

❦

Opening Ourselves to Change

The Samaritan Woman Opens Herself to Change

In Jesus' day a popular Rabbi's saying went, "The water of Samaria is more unclean than the blood of swine." Another adage warned that no Israelite should eat of anything that is a Samaritan's, "for it is as if he should eat swine's flesh." Jesus broke long-standing religious, racial, and gender barriers the day he walked into Samaria and met a woman at a well.

When King Solomon died around 930 B.C., the nation of Israel split into two kingdoms. The Northern and Southern Kingdoms feuded continually. Hatred intensified after the Assyrian conquest of the Northern Kingdom of Israel in 722 B.C. The Assyrian conquerors sent citizens to intermarry with the few survivors of northern Israel. Samaritans were the descendants of these mixed marriages. They were considered unclean and were hated by the Jews.

"True Jews" shunned the "mixed" race. Most Jewish worshipers traveled out of their way to bypass Samaria en route to Jerusalem. They chose the longer route, despite the rougher journey on hot, dusty roads. Those Jewish pilgrims who opted to cross Samaria on a quicker route to Jerusalem ran the risk of being attacked by bands of Samaritans.

Jesus, however, not only led his followers through Samaria, but he stayed there for two days! Jesus stopped along the roadside outside of a Samaritan city called Sychar, near the plot of ground Jacob had given to his son Joseph. He sent his disciples ahead for food while he rested at Jacob's well.

As Jesus sat beside the well in the heat of the day, a woman came to draw water. It was unusual for a Samaritan woman to be there in the afternoon. Customarily, women walked to the well in groups in early morning or at twilight to avoid the worst heat of the day. That this woman came alone at noon indicates she was ostracized, considered immoral by her community. Later Jesus pointed out why the woman was considered immoral: *"You have had five husbands, and the one you have now is not your husband"* (John 4:18).

A Jewish man did not speak to a woman in public, and certainly not to an immoral woman. Yet Jesus not only spoke to the Samaritan woman at the well, he asked her for a drink.

Amazed, the woman responded, *"How is it that you, a Jew, ask a drink of me, a woman of Samaria?"* (John 4:9). The rest of the verse gives part of the explanation for her astonishment: *Jews do not share things in common with Samaritans.*

When the disciples returned from their errand, they must have been shocked to see their master conversing with a Samaritan. They had no love for Samaritans. In fact, later when the disciples were shunned by Samaritans on a return trip through Samaria, James and John asked for permission to command fire to come down from heaven and consume the Samaritans (Luke 9:51-56).

Yet finding Jesus talking with a Samaritan wasn't what bothered the disciples the most. What they were most astonished and disturbed about was the fact that *he was speaking with a woman* (John 4:27).

What Jesus said to the Samaritan woman changed her. He told her all about herself. Then Jesus told her all about himself. *"But the hour is coming, and is now here, when the true worshipers will worship the Father in spirit and truth, for the Father seeks such as these to worship him"* (John 4:23). The woman at the well opened herself to become the kind of worshiper the Father seeks.

The Samaritan woman might have ignored Jesus. She might have refused to believe that she could change. Instead, she listened to

Jesus and to what he had to offer. She came to the well for water; she left with the promise of living water from the Messiah. She came to the well alone, cut off from her community. She returned bringing her community with her to Christ. The Samaritan woman might have refused to talk about herself or the Messiah. Instead, she opened herself to change, and Christ changed her.

Today's Changed Women

Just as the Samaritan woman opened herself to change, we need to be open to change. Leslie's life was transformed by an unexpected request. Leslie used and sold drugs in South Central Los Angeles. When a Christian couple moved into the neighborhood, Leslie was suspicious. She would have rejected any attempt made to help her. But the Christian woman surprised Leslie by asking for her help. "She asked me to show her where the good stores were. I was so shocked she'd ask me for something, I said yes." Saying yes was Leslie's first step toward being open to change. Eventually Leslie renewed a faith in Christ and changed her life.

Like Leslie, Nan discovered she needed to be open to change. Nan and her in-laws were suspicious of each other because of their different backgrounds. After a year of avoiding each other, they admitted their suspicions. Nan was determined to open herself up to her in-laws. "When I finally decided I wanted things to change so much that I was willing to change, I began to understand them. I began to appreciate them and their love for my husband." Nan's mother-in-law responded with a reciprocal understanding. They changed because they opened themselves to change.

Rose grew up in a Mexican-American neighborhood in Chicago. "I knew I was prejudiced against the blacks in my school. Even after I became a Christian, I was afraid of African-Americans. I started to believe that my prejudice was too ingrained, that I'd never get over it. It wasn't until I opened up to one African-American girl in my class, that I started to see a difference. I asked her to help me with algebra. She looked shocked, but she helped me. We've become friends." Like the woman at the well, Rose and her friend crossed the boundaries of culture and race.

The Samaritan woman didn't let her circumstances seal her fate. She opened herself to the possibility of change, and Christ changed her. Christ can change us, too.

Bonding with Our Sister, the Woman at the Well

The Samaritan woman opened herself to Jesus and to change. If we want to change, our first step is to open ourselves to Christ and to other people. Write down anything that keeps you from opening yourself to change. Are you suspicious of another culture or race? Are you closed to ideas that come from certain groups of people? This week take a step across that man-made barrier. Introduce yourself to, or take time to talk with, someone you've been avoiding. Like our sister, the Samaritan woman, open yourself to learning and to change.

11

∞

Getting to Know Ourselves

The Samaritan Woman's Self-Revelation

The Samaritan woman's personality comes across from the moment she enters the scene. She's spunky, quick, possibly flirtatious. Although surprised a Jewish man would speak to her and ask her for a drink of water, she was not speechless. She held up her end of the conversation with intelligence and wit. During their talk, Jesus forced her to take a hard look at herself. And seeing her true self changed her forever.

The dramatic point of change in the conversation at the well comes with an answer that seems to have no relation to the question. The woman asked Jesus to give her the living water that would save her from daily journeys to the well. To this request, Jesus said, *"Go, call your husband, and come back"* (John 4:16). At first look, Jesus' response seems to have nothing to do with what they've been discussing. But this question leads the woman to a dramatic point of self-revelation.

When the woman replied that she had no husband, Jesus said, *"You are right in saying, 'I have no husband'; for you have had five husbands, and the one you have now is not your husband"* (John 4:17-18). The woman may have been married five times, or she may have been a prostitute. Either she hadn't admitted her own moral condition or she chose to ignore it. Jesus wanted her to face herself honestly.

The Samaritan woman didn't want to discuss her personal life, so she quickly tried to erect a barrier. She resorted to an old religious contention: *"Our ancestors worshiped on this mountain, but you say that the place where people must worship is in Jerusalem"* (John 4:20).

Jesus sidestepped the Samaritan woman's attempts to change the subject. Where she worshiped was not the issue. He moved her to a personal, spiritual truth: *"The true worshipers will worship the Father in spirit and truth"* (John 4:23). Jesus called her to face the truth about herself.

There's an intricate connection between seeing ourselves honestly, admitting our weaknesses, and living in Christ's strength. Romans 3:23 says, *All have sinned and fall short of the glory of God.* The Greek word for sin here is an archery term for "missed the mark." If we confront ourselves, we have to admit we miss the mark of God's highest standards; we need God's grace.

Self-revelation also helps us understand forgiveness. Jesus didn't reveal the Samaritan woman's sin so that he could point a finger and condemn her. He was waiting for her to see herself clearly so that he could offer compassion and forgiveness. When she could learn to love and accept herself, then she could love and accept others who still condemned her.

Today's Women Changed by Self-Revelation

Because seeing ourselves accurately usually involves a degree of pain or regret, we may fight self-revelation by building barriers as our Samaritan sister did. The easiest barrier we can throw up when someone challenges us spiritually is the religious quarrel. This is what the Samaritan woman did when she asked Jesus who had the right spot for worship. This is also what a young married couple discovered they were doing themselves. In three years of marriage, Craig, a Catholic, and Jenny, a Lutheran, had not attended church. Jenny admitted, "I can see now that Craig and I weren't so much avoiding the church argument as we were avoiding God." Once they admitted their spiritual problem, they were able to overcome their religious differences and find a church where they both felt they could worship.

It's not easy to confront ourselves with complete honesty. Alison had a successful career in medicine, but there were things in her life she didn't like to confront. "I grew up in a dysfunctional family where I was criticized at every turn. Once I made the mistake of telling my mother I got nervous at school spelling matches. She was angry and disappointed with me, so I felt disappointed in myself. I learned never to let down my guard, even to myself. I'm only now discovering the power in admitting my faults."

Another woman who has learned the benefits of honest introspection is Laurie, a thirty-two-year-old kindergarten teacher. Laurie's relationship with Christ changed when she began to understand her shortcomings and God's forgiveness. "I never felt close to Christ," said Laurie, "until I understood myself and my need for Christ's forgiveness. I hadn't committed any of the 'biggie' sins— murder, adultery, idol worship—so I felt pretty good about my life. But I had to admit I'd passed along a juicy bit of gossip. And if I didn't commit horrible acts, I certainly didn't do everything I knew I should either. Admitting my shortcomings helped me see my need for Christ."

Ruby, a wonderful Christian woman who has raised eleven children, would agree with Laurie. Ruby said, "My best times with my Lord have come when I'm at my lowest. When I feel dirty inside, Jesus comes like water washing over me."

Once we see where we fall short, we can ask Christ for the strength to change. Paul wrote, *I can do all things through him who strengthens me* (Philippians 4:13).

We need to imitate our Samaritan sister's honesty and inquisitiveness. Are we free to let God and others reveal to us what we're really like? The woman at the well changed and became an influential disciple. She ran to tell the people in the nearby villages about the Messiah: *"Come see a man who told me everything I have ever done"* (John 4:39). They came because she had been changed, not by argument, but by revelation.

Bonding with Our Sister, the Woman at the Well

God wants us to offer every part of our being to God. That means we need to know ourselves, our strengths and weaknesses. The woman at the well was able to change because Jesus helped her to take an honest look at her life. Prayerfully ask God to search your heart and reveal to you more of yourself. Write down at least twelve specific things you want to change in yourself or your life. Pray every morning for strength to see yourself clearly. Then pray for the power to act out those changes all day. Thank God every night for helping you change.

12

∞

Getting to Know Jesus

The Samaritan Woman's Encounter with Christ

At Jacob's well the Samaritan woman talked to Jesus. Through that conversation, she came to know herself better and understand her need for the living water Jesus offered. More importantly, the Samaritan woman came to know Jesus. That knowledge of Christ changed her.

Jesus started his conversation with the Samaritan by meeting her where she was—on the physical plane. He was thirsty, and he asked her for a drink. Then he slowly led the woman to a deeper, spiritual understanding of the living water he offered.

When Jesus promised living water, the Samaritan woman quickly pointed out the physical realities: He had no bucket. The well was deep. He could not be greater than Jacob, whose children and flocks drank regular water from the well. Besides, what was living water? Where would he get such a thing?

Jesus offered himself as the answer to her questions and to her problems. Jesus cared enough about the Samaritan woman to reveal himself to her at a time when he hadn't yet fully declared himself to the world. He knew that her only hope for change was knowing him as Messiah.

Today's Changed Women Encounter Christ

Jesus began with what the woman of Samaria thought she needed—water that would keep her from having to return to the well. Then he showed the woman her real need—to know him as the Messiah. People come to Christ initially for many reasons: death of a loved one, failure in life, desire for something more. Those needs lead us to our real need—to know Christ.

When we have a problem, like our Samaritan sister, we may find it hard to get past the physical reality to discover our true need. Last Thanksgiving Eve I came home from a hard day and found one kid sick, one obnoxious, and one grouchy. Then I opened the mail: Uncle Sam announcing an audit, the phone company demanding a subsidy, three bills that couldn't be paid until after Christmas, and the library claiming I'd lost two books.

No matter what solutions I came up with, they were followed by a "Yes, but." (Yes, but then we'll owe interest. Yes, but how can I prove I returned the books?) I couldn't get beyond the physical realities to see that what I needed was Jesus. When I finally took time out to pray, I was able to shift my focus to Christ and gain perspective on my physical problems.

Carla, who home schools second, fourth, and seventh graders, shares the experience of being changed by the knowledge of Christ. She talks about three ways she's tried to get peace . . . of a sort. "I can work hard, do everything on my list, sit down and breathe deeply. But that peace only lasts a couple of seconds, until I think of enough work for a whole new list. Then there's the peace I try to psych myself into, telling myself nothing is worth worrying about. That rarely works. The peace I need is in Christ. I only get it when I give him my worries. Then I find I'm free to let Christ change the way I'm looking at my problems."

In the same way, Corrine believes her change of attitude has come from a deeper relationship with Christ. Corrine began to know Christ three years ago when she was twenty-seven. "Sometimes a gratitude sweeps over me. I remember that powerless feeling of wanting to change but not being able to. I was cranky, irritable, critical of everybody—not that everyone saw me that way. That's how I felt. Now I still get cranky, but I have access to the power that can change me. I know Christ!"

Knowledge of Christ changed the Samaritan woman. She left her water vessel and the physical water she'd come for. Filled with the living water of the Spirit and the knowledge of Jesus as Messiah, she ran to the village to tell everyone about the Messiah. She moved from isolation to community and led her people to see this Messiah for themselves.

Psalm 46:10 says, *Be still, and know that I am God!* The way to *peace of God, which surpasses all understanding* (Philippians 4:7) is Jesus, *the way, and the truth, and the life* (John 14:6). The more we know Christ, the clearer is our need for him. If we want to change, we need to know Christ.

How do we get to know Christ? The Samaritan woman was able to talk with Jesus face to face and let Jesus reveal himself to her. We can get to know Christ by letting him reveal himself to us in the scriptures, in prayer, and in fellowship with his other children.

The apostle Paul, who changed dramatically when he came to know Christ, wrote, *I regard everything as loss because of the surpassing value of knowing Christ Jesus my Lord* (Philippians 3:8). What was true for the woman at the well, is true for us. Nothing is more important, more life-changing than a knowledge of Christ!

Bonding with Our Sister, the Woman at the Well

If we have come to know Christ, then like the woman at the well we have changed. List five specific ways your life has changed as a result of knowing Christ. Now describe what your life might look like if you knew Christ more deeply. What might you give up or take on? Finally, list three things you can do this week to give yourself a chance to know Christ better: have regular devotions or quiet times, go for walks, call a Christian friend, go to church or a Bible study, pray every time you get behind the wheel of a car, etc. Now, do whatever it takes to grow in your relationship with Christ. Bond with your Samaritan sister, the woman at the well. Let Jesus come to you and help you change as he helped her.

A Prayer for Change

Dear Lord, thank you for the power to become a changed woman. Help me listen to you and—like the woman at the well—open myself to change. I pray your Spirit would guide me into truth about myself. Use me to bring others to see you, know you, and be changed by you.

Mary of Bethany

Now as they went on their way, he [Jesus] entered a certain village, where a woman named Martha welcomed him into her home. She had a sister named Mary, who sat at the Lord's feet and listened to what he was saying. But Martha was distracted by her many tasks; so she came to him and asked, "Lord, do you not care that my sister has left me to do all the work by myself? Tell her then to help me." But the Lord answered her, "Martha, Martha, you are worried and distracted by many things; there is need of only one thing. Mary has chosen the better part, which will not be taken away from her." (Luke 10:38-42)

Now a certain man was ill, Lazarus of Bethany, the village of Mary and her sister Martha. Mary was the one who anointed the Lord with perfume and wiped his feet with her hair; her brother Lazarus was ill. (John 11:1-2)

Mary took a pound of costly perfume made of pure nard, anointed Jesus' feet, and wiped them with her hair. The house was filled with the fragrance of the perfume. . . . Jesus said, "Leave her alone. She bought it so that she might keep it for the day of my burial." (John 12:3, 7)

13

∞

Seasons of Growth

Mary of Bethany's Growing Faith

Jesus Christ left his home in heaven when he came to earth. *"Foxes have holes,"* he said, *"and birds of the air have nests; but the Son of Man has nowhere to lay his head"* (Luke 9:58). As Jesus traveled with his disciples, he found a home away from home in Bethany, a suburb of Jerusalem about two miles from the eastern slope of the Mount of Olives. There Jesus stayed with a family of siblings: Mary, her sister Martha, and their brother Lazarus.

Jesus' friendship with Mary and Martha must have amazed his contemporaries. For a rabbi to teach a woman in a home setting was unheard of. It was suspect for a man to enter a woman's home or even to be in the same room with a woman who was not a relation. Men seldom allowed women to eat with them. Yet Jesus stayed with Martha and Mary, ate with them, wept with them, and loved them.

The Bible gives us three scenes that include Mary of Bethany: two dinners and Lazarus' death. In between the two dinners Mary experienced a tough season of growth. She learned a hard lesson in waiting and trusting when her brother, Lazarus died.

Imagine you're Mary. Your brother lies sick and very close to death. But you know the answer! Jesus is your friend, and he loves your brother. Jesus has healed hundreds of strangers. Surely he will heal your Lazarus.

You send word to Jesus. *"Lord, he whom you love is ill"* (John 11:3). That ought to do it. Surely Jesus will drop whatever he is doing and rush to Lazarus' bedside to make everything all right.

You wait, and you pray. Any moment now you expect a knock on your door. You wait and wait and wait. Martha probably busies herself recleaning the house, maybe preparing a meal, getting Jesus' room ready in case he stays over.

Two days pass, and Lazarus grows worse. Someone reminds you of what happened with the centurion and his slave in Capernaum. That time Jesus didn't even have to come and see the paralyzed servant. Jesus healed him over a long distance. But Lazarus, instead of improving, suffers more. Where is Jesus?

John records what Jesus did when he heard about Lazarus' illness: *Accordingly, though Jesus loved Martha and her sister and Lazarus, after having heard that Lazarus was ill, he stayed two days longer in the place where he was* (John 11:5-6). Jesus stayed where he was two days then traveled perhaps another two days to get to Bethany!

You watch your brother grow sicker and sicker . . . and finally die. You and your sister bury Lazarus and go into mourning. You feel Jesus let your brother die. What would you do the next time you saw Jesus?

The Bible says that Mary ran to Jesus the next time she saw him. When Jesus finally arrived outside of Bethany, Mary ran to meet him. John gives us a glimpse of Mary's inner turmoil. *When Mary came where Jesus was and saw him, she knelt at his feet and said to him, "Lord, if you had been here, my brother would not have died." When Jesus saw her weeping, and the Jews who came with her also weeping, he was greatly disturbed in spirit and deeply moved* (John 11:32-33)

Mary's cry sounds like an affirmation and an accusation. Jesus could have kept Lazarus alive, but he didn't. Instead, Mary had to wait. That waiting hurt Mary, and Jesus was very moved when he saw her mourning. But Christ had bigger plans that Mary didn't yet understand. Jesus brought her brother back to life right before Mary's eyes! Mary's hard season of waiting gave her an opportunity to see a miracle.

If Christ makes us wait as he did Mary, it is because he has something greater in mind. We don't always understand why we have to wait, but if we pay attention as our sister Mary did, those difficult waiting periods become seasons of growth during which God can change us.

Today's Changed Women of Growing Faith

Nobody likes to wait, but everyone has to wait. How we handle waiting periods may determine whether we'll give up or, as Mary did, grow in faith.

Joan, now fifty, waited fifteen years for a child. "I prayed, and sometimes I felt my words bounce back at me as month after month went by and I still wasn't pregnant. I was almost forty when Jessica was born. God knew I needed those extra years to grow into the kind of mother Jess would need." Waiting periods can be our best opportunities to grow in Christ.

Dian had a similar waiting period, with a different outcome. "For seven years my life was a roller coaster, praying but not getting pregnant. Last year my husband and I adopted a little boy. Now I'm so glad God stuck to his guns and made us wait! I don't know what I'd do without Micah!"

Other women have to wait—for the right job opportunity, the right man, the right dream. Jennifer is the young mother of Bridget, a special needs child. Her toughest waiting season came when Bridget had a three-hour seizure. Bridget was flown to a children's hospital, where she remained on life support for two weeks. Jennifer said, "I have never been closer to God than I was while my baby was in the hospital." Bridget recovered, but Jennifer has never forgotten her season of growth.

Each waiting period—no matter the outcome—offers us a chance for growth. If we follow the example of Mary of Bethany, we'll grow in faith during our seasons of waiting on God.

Bonding with Our Sister, Mary of Bethany

Mary of Bethany had to wait for God in a tough season of growth. What do you think Jesus taught Mary by making her wait? Think of five things you have had to wait for in your life. Include things you waited for but never received. Beside each, write what you learned during the waiting period. Were any of those waiting periods seasons of growth? Next, write down anything you are waiting for now. Just as God taught Mary of Bethany during her waiting period, what might God want to teach you as you wait?

14

∞

The Priority of Listening

Mary of Bethany, the Listener

After long days of talking in parables to people who didn't always understand, Jesus must have enjoyed his retreats to Bethany. There he knew he would find a woman who had ears to hear, a disciple eager to catch every word, every nuance. Mary of Bethany had learned the priority of listening: *Now as they went on their way, he [Jesus] entered a certain village, where a woman named Martha welcomed him into her home. She had a sister named Mary, who sat at the Lord's feet and listened to what he was saying. But Martha was distracted by her many tasks; so she came to him and asked, "Lord, do you not care that my sister has left me to do all the work by myself? Tell her then to help me"* (Luke 10:38-40).

Probably the apostles and everyone else present expected Jesus to agree with Martha. Jesus surprised them: *"Martha, Martha, you are worried and distracted by many things; there is need of only one thing. Mary has chosen the better part, which will not be taken away from her"* (Luke 10:41-42). Mary had discovered the priority of listening to Christ.

While her sister, Martha, scurried around with dinner preparations, Mary *sat at the Lord's feet and listened to what he was saying.* The term "at his feet" expresses the humility and receptivity of discipleship. Mary knew nothing was more important than giving Jesus her full attention. Martha was serving Jesus in her own way, but Mary made listening to Jesus her priority.

When Martha asked Jesus to make Mary help with dinner, Jesus may have answered her with a good-natured pun. He told Martha she was too worried with various dishes, but only one portion was necessary. Mary chose the best "one portion"—undistracted devotion to Christ.

Many of the distractions that compete with our devotion are in themselves good things. What would have been wrong with Mary's helping her sister serve dinner? The disciples were right; the valuable jar of perfume Mary used to anoint Jesus could have been traded for food to help poor people. It's hard to answer Martha's and the disciples' complaints because they seem so logical. Yet there are times when devotion supersedes logic. Mary knew how to say no to good choices and yes to the one best thing.

Jesus promised that the one best portion wouldn't be taken from Mary. Material choices will deteriorate, but what Mary took from Jesus would last and grow inside her. Mary might lose her money, her home, her brother, but she'd never lose the wisdom she learned at Jesus' feet. Our sister Mary became an effective disciple because she understood the priority of listening to Jesus.

Today's Listening Women

Why don't we always give God our full attention as Mary of Bethany did? One reason we may not always have ears to hear is that we don't value what we're listening to. We don't expect it to affect us, and therefore it doesn't.

Krystal used to hate it when her husband watched the evening news. "At the end of the hour, I couldn't have repeated one news item. But after Frank [her husband] was sent into military action, all of a sudden I started caring about politics. I knew as much about that war as Dan Rather."

Krystal's listening changed when she placed a higher value on what she heard. Jesus told his disciples in Mark 4:23-4, *"Let anyone with ears to hear listen! Pay attention to what you hear; the measure you give will be the measure you get, and still more will be given you."*

What we put into listening is what we get out. We need to value what Christ says to us in the Bible and through prayer. We need to value what we hear as highly as Mary of Bethany valued every word Jesus said to her.

So many dishes demand our attention; it's hard to focus on the one important portion, our devotion to Christ. If I want to know what distractions are interfering with my devotion, all I have to do is pray. I may begin in earnest worship, but before long, various dishes run through my mind. How will I meet my deadline? What will we have for dinner? How can I arrange volleyball transportation for my daughter? I need to change my thinking and concentrate on the *one portion*, Christ.

Abbie is an attractive, single mother of three and a business executive. She confessed she's no stranger to distractions. "Why is it I sit through entire church services and never get a thing out of it?" Abbie asked. Then she sighed and admitted, "Okay, I usually have a million things on my mind, and it's hard for anything else to break through." Before church, Abbie writes down all possible distractions and offers her list to God in prayer. Then she tries to focus on worshiping God.

Mary of Bethany listened intently to Jesus. If we follow the example of this sister in Christ, we too will become listening disciples.

Bonding with Our Sister, Mary of Bethany

On a sheet of paper, make three columns with the following headings: Various Dishes (Concerns), Solutions, and Listening Plans. Use the first column to make a list of the various dishes on your plate this week that may interfere with your undistracted devotion to Christ (concerns, jobs, errands, relationships). In the next column write down any solutions to those dishes. (Are there some items you can erase and let go?) Finally, in the last column, write at least three ways you'll listen to Jesus as Mary did (for example, Bible study, praying while driving, saying no to one distraction). Like our sister Mary of Bethany, make listening to God a priority.

15

∞

Who's Watching?

Mary of Bethany's Devotion

Mary of Bethany must have learned how to tune out other people when they tried to keep her from listening to and serving Christ. She didn't alter her devotion to Christ for fear of what others might think. Mary recognized an audience of one: Jesus.

We can only imagine the pressure Martha and Mary must have been under when they learned Jesus and his disciples were going to be their guests. We can understand Martha's preoccupation with preparations. Mary showed a different kind of hospitality, however. She focused on her guest. The only person Mary cared about pleasing was Jesus. She must have known Martha would criticize her for not helping with dinner. But Mary wasn't acting for other people; she was serving Jesus.

Because Mary had chosen God as her audience, she was able to show undistracted devotion to Christ. After Lazarus died, mourners gathered around Mary. When she heard that Jesus was close to the village, she got up, ignored all mourning etiquette, made no excuses to the confounded mourners, and ran. She reached Jesus before he arrived in Bethany. Mary was not afraid to weep and pour out her feelings. And before Jesus raised her brother from the dead, he wept with her.

In a final act of uninhibited devotion, Mary anointed Christ with costly oil and wiped off the excess with her hair. *Mary took a pound of costly perfume made of pure nard, anointed Jesus' feet, and wiped them with her hair* (John 12:3).

Nard was the plant that furnished essence for perfume; pure nard was the most expensive form. Normally a woman or a servant washed the feet of guests, who every day walked the dusty roads. Mary washed Jesus' feet with such generosity that not only did she use valuable perfume for the job, but she wiped off the excess oil with her hair.

For a woman to let down her hair in public was a scandalous act. A Jewish woman of that time prided herself on never letting anyone but her husband see her hair. Yet Mary was only concerned with devoting herself to Christ. If that meant using her hair to wipe off the extra oil from Jesus' feet, she would let down her hair and use it as a rag. It was Christ who mattered, not the conventions of society or what other people might say about her.

Today's Devoted Women

Today we need to devote ourselves to Christ as our sister Mary of Bethany devoted herself. Most of us have to play hostess now and then and can identify with Jane's experience. "I hate to admit it," Jane said, "but I actually enjoy our time with my mother-in-law more than weekends at Mom's. Mom goes to so much trouble getting ready for us and feeding us; I hardly even see her. Dick's mom stocks up on cold cuts and lets us fend for ourselves so we have more time to visit with her."

What motivates you when guests come to your house? Do you want to make sure everyone knows you're a great cook and house-keeper? Or does your hospitality, like Mary's, focus on giving your undivided attention to your guests?

Living for Christ, rather than for other people, may require us to make tough choices. A.J. graduated from Yale and turned down scholarships for graduate study because she wanted to be a mission-ary. "The hardest thing I've ever done was telling my parents and my friends that I had decided to go to Albania. They weren't pleased, but they weren't the ones I was trying to please."

Paul wrote to the Galatians (1:10), *Am I now seeking human approval, or God's approval? Or am I trying to please people? If I were still pleasing people, I would not be a servant of Christ.* God is our audience.

Are we free, like Mary of Bethany, to do the unexpected for Christ, to risk looking foolish? Trisha talks about a woman she used to work with who sang hymns every day while getting ready to open the department store. "She knew we made fun of her, but she didn't care. She was singing for God." Trisha has never forgotten the image of that woman who had chosen to devote herself to Christ.

2 Corinthians 5:13 says, *For if we are beside ourselves, it is for God; if we are in our right mind, it is for you.* If God is our audience, it won't matter what others think.

After the anointing, Jesus made a promise involving Mary: *"Truly I tell you, wherever this good news is proclaimed in the whole world, what she has done will be told in remembrance of her"* (Matthew 26:13). It's ironic that this woman who wanted no audience but God was given the world as an audience.

Bonding with Our Sister, Mary of Bethany

Mary of Bethany was devoted to Jesus. She lived her life for him. Make a list of areas in your life where you care too much about what others think. (Hospitality? Job? What kind of person you appear to be to others?) What would you do differently if no one but God saw you?

A Prayer for Spiritual Growth

Lord, help me to grow as my sister Mary of Bethany did. Change me into a listening disciple who pleases you in everything. I confess that there are areas of my life where I care too much about what other people think. I confess that I am distracted by so many things every day. Help me to concentrate on the one good thing, you in me. Make me as devoted as Mary of Bethany. Amen.

The Hemorrhaging Woman

As he went, the crowds pressed in on him. Now there was a woman who had been suffering from hemorrhages for twelve years; and though she had spent all she had on physicians, no one could cure her. She came up behind him and touched the fringe of his clothes, and immediately her hemorrhage stopped. Then Jesus asked, "Who touched me?" When all denied it, Peter said, "Master, the crowds surround you and press in on you." But Jesus said, "Someone touched me; for I noticed that power had gone out from me." When the woman saw that she could not remain hidden, she came trembling; and falling down before him, she declared in the presence of all the people why she had touched him, and how she had been immediately healed. He said to her, "Daughter, your faith has made you well; go in peace." (Luke 8:42-48)

16

❦

"Daughter"

The Hemorrhaging Woman Becomes a Daughter

By the time Jesus came through Capernaum, the hemorrhaging Israelite woman was living alone. For twelve years she had bled constantly, a uterine or menstrual bleeding that cut her off from her society. For twelve long years she had been untouchable. If she had ever married, she would now probably be divorced. No man could risk touching her in her condition. If she had lived with family, they had likely kicked her out. Her physical, social, religious, and economic problems made her an outcast. Her encounter with Jesus would change everything.

Physically the woman suffered. Only in our nightmares can we imagine what it would be like to have a menstrual period last twelve years! She was weakened by her continual menstruation, and she had no iron supplements, no estrogen additives. This woman also had no modern washing machine. Much of her time would have been spent with the hygienic necessities of everyday life, the washing and rewashing of her soiled menstrual cloths.

Besides her physical torment, the hemorrhaging woman was ostracized from society. According to laws set up in Leviticus 15:19-30, a woman was "unclean" while she had her period. She could not take part in celebrations or social functions.

Not only was a menstruating woman unclean, but anyone who touched or was touched by her was also declared unclean. It's likely that no one had even touched this poor woman for twelve years. Yet the social ostracism ran even deeper. Everything a menstruating woman touched, sat on, or lay on was defiled. If someone came to her house and sat on one of her chairs, that person would become unclean. If the woman entered the house of a friend, the friend would have to wash everything that might have been touched. Even the friend remained defiled until evening.

Luke, a physician himself, tells us that the outcast woman was also economically bankrupt. She had spent all that she had trying to be healed; yet she was no better, and in fact she grew worse.

Perhaps the worst form of rejection she experienced was rejection from public worship. This woman of such amazing faith could not go to the temple or the local synagogue. She could no longer participate in family celebrations of holy days and great feasts. She might pray alone in her room, but group fellowship and worship were denied her. Twelve years. For twelve years she experienced all this pain, ostracism, and loneliness.

When Jesus came along, the hemorrhaging woman pushed through the crowd, arms outstretched, until she could just reach the hem of his coat. As soon as she touched it, the woman was healed. She knew it! She felt it! The twelve-year issue of blood stopped immediately and completely.

This woman had been rejected for so long, she expected condemnation. She was unclean, and she realized she had defiled Jesus and many others. She had also stopped the procession on its way to Jairus' house to heal his daughter. What if Jesus didn't reach Jairus' sick child in time? And so she hid. She hid until she heard the voice of Jesus telling her to come out.

Instead of condemning the woman, Jesus turned to her and said, *"Daughter, your faith has made you well; go in peace"* (Luke 8:48).

"Daughter."

There is no more intimate name Jesus could have used for this woman who remains unnamed in Scripture. The hemorrhaging woman went from a woman rejected to a woman loved, in that one word—daughter.

John wrote, *See what love the Father has given us that we should be called children of God. . . . And all who have this hope in him purify themselves just as he is pure* (I John 3:1, 3). This daughter was changed, purified by the touch and love of Christ.

Today's Changed Daughters

The hemorrhaging woman felt her acceptance when Jesus called her "daughter." We still need to realize God's love and acceptance of us as daughters.

For eight years Bonnie suffered from endometriosis and uterine bleeding. "There's a sickness you get from feeling tired so long," she explained. My King James Version Bible calls patience, *longsuffering*. Suffering a long time takes a lot of patience!" Bonnie takes advantage of modern medications not available to the hemorrhaging woman. Yet she relies on Christ every day for her strength. She added, "I have to ask God for help as many as a hundred times a day."

Bonnie suffers physically. Margo, a physically strong woman in her early twenties, experiences a different kind of pain. She feels a kind of social ostracism when she visits her parents. "I grew up in this town and deserved my bad reputation. But I've straightened out. Still, when I return, people treat me like they think I'll contaminate them." Margo reminds herself that she is a daughter of the King, even when people don't treat her like royalty.

Sensing still another form of rejection, Debbie tried to hold back tears as she explained how unacceptable she felt. "I walked into the post office and saw two F.B.I. posters marked: WANTED. I pictured my ugly mug up next to them, but my heading would read UNWANTED." Overweight and scarred from acne, Debbie felt physically unacceptable. She's still trying to grasp the greatness of God's love, love that counts her a daughter.

The hemorrhaging woman must have felt loved and accepted when Jesus called her "daughter." Today we need a fresh understanding of God's love and acceptance. We are God's daughters, too.

Bonding with Our Sister, the Hemorrhaging Woman

As daughters of God, we are sisters of the hemorrhaging woman. Meditate on what it means to be God's daughter. For each of the following stages of childhood, list what parents are expected to do for their children (I've suggested a few ideas to get you started.): Unborn Child in the Womb (ex. prepare nursery); Infant (ex. provide all basic needs); Toddler (ex. teach to talk, walk); School-age (ex. help learn, model behavior); Teen (ex. help build responsibility); Adult (ex. advise, support). Meditate on what each relationship means to you as a daughter of God. Thank God for taking such excellent care of you.

17

⚭

Accepting Other Daughters

The Hemorrhaging Woman and Her Community

When Jesus met the hemorrhaging woman, he was on his way to heal Jairus' daughter. Jairus was at the top of the social ladder; the hemorrhaging woman was on the bottom rung. She halted the entire procession when she reached out and touched the hem of Jesus' garment. Then she hid. She was healed. She had received what she came for. If Jesus hadn't demanded to know who had touched him, would the woman have come out of hiding?

Jesus called her out. *"Who touched me?"* he asked. The woman had been found out! What would happen to her now? She fell down trembling before Jesus and confessed she was the one who had touched him. Then she told all the people what Jesus had done for her—she had been healed. *She declared in the presence of all the people why she had touched him, and how she had been immediately healed* (Luke 8:47).

This woman had been ostracized by many of the people in the crowd. Now Jesus had healed her and accepted her as a daughter. In turn, she came out of hiding and testified to the crowd. Her gratitude overflowed. She declared in front of everyone what Jesus had done for her.

Today's Women in Community

The feeling of not fitting in, not being wanted, being untouchable can take root and fester inside us. If we can understand what it means to be accepted by Christ, to be called daughter, then we can come out of hiding as the hemorrhaging woman did. We can turn to the crowds and tell them what Christ has done for us.

Theresa had always felt socially unacceptable. Although attractive and still in her late twenties, Theresa had never overcome painful shyness. "I could sit next to someone at an office party, and the next day at work they would ask me why I didn't make it to the party." Through counseling and help from church friends, Theresa grew to understand God's acceptance. Although she would still call herself shy, Theresa learned to start up conversations and hold her own in discussions. She explained the difficulty she still had with her co-workers. "Now that I could talk to them or reach out to them, I wasn't sure I wanted to. Some of them had mocked me for four years. But I knew what Christ would have done, and that's what I did. I accepted them and tried to let Christ's love flow through me to the people I work with. One woman at work said, 'What happened to you, Theresa? You've changed.' All I had to do was tell her who changed me!"

All around us are people who feel rejected. Since Christ has accepted us, we cannot help but be grateful and accept others. Nobody is beyond the scope of our acceptance. Peter had to learn to accept the Gentiles he had always rejected. *"God has shown me that I should not call anyone profane or unclean"* (Acts 10:28).

Christ loved us enough to die for us even though we are sinners. We didn't earn our way into God's good graces. Isaiah wrote, *And all our righteous deeds are like a filthy cloth* (64:6), comparing our best efforts to soiled menstrual rags (literal translation).

Jesus knows our weaknesses, our apathy to anyone's problems but our own, our unwillingness to give money or time generously. He knows our worst thoughts. Yet Christ accepts us as he accepted the hemorrhaging woman, and he tells us, "Go in peace." Christ's love should make us want to pass this peace on to others.

Many single women and women whose husbands don't attend church feel a kind of religious rejection. "I've gone to the same Bible school class for thirteen years," said Lou Ann. "But since Ron died, I feel like an outsider there." A newly divorced mom told me, "I don't want to go to the singles' functions at church, but I feel uneasy around couples."

Another woman, Evelyn, middle-aged and middle-income, told me, "I used to sit alone in church and feel everyone must know how alone I felt. Then I'd overhear couples talking about having dinner together. I wanted them to invite me." The neighbors of the hemorrhaging woman didn't think they were cruel to her. They just kept their distance. But isn't that a form of cruelty? If we feel accepted by Christ, God's love should overflow to others through us.

Paul wrote, *For I am convinced that neither death, nor life, nor angels, nor rulers, nor things present, nor things to come, nor powers, nor height, nor depth, nor anything else in all creation, will be able to separate us from the love of God in Christ Jesus our Lord* (Romans 8:38-39). The hemorrhaging woman felt that love when she met Jesus. Just as she did, we can accept Christ's love, come out of hiding, and pass that love on to others.

Bonding with Our Sister, the Hemorrhaging Woman

What makes you feel unacceptable today? Write down everything you can think of. Now turn each "flaw" over to Christ and thank him that he accepts you completely, just as he accepted the hemorrhaging woman. But don't stop there. Picture one person, someone you think is lonely. Let God's acceptance of you overflow to that person. What can you do today to help her or him? Take time to listen to others as Jesus listened to the hemorrhaging woman. Accepting is not merely thinking nice thoughts about someone or talking to her occasionally. It means taking on friendship—inviting people into our lives, sharing ourselves and our talents with them. Let Christ heal you as he healed the hemorrhaging woman.

18

∞

Uncomfortable Faith

The Hemorrhaging Woman's Risky Faith

After twelve years of rejection and failure, the hemorrhaging woman might have felt safer and more comfortable staying at home feeling sorry for herself. It would take great emotional strength to leave her sanctuary and go out into the society that rejected her. She would have to rally all her physical strength to walk and find Jesus. When she did find him, Jesus wasn't standing still, chatting with friends. A crowd surrounded him as he rushed to save the life of an important synagogue leader's child. Even if the hemorrhaging woman did succeed in touching Jesus, wouldn't the crowd condemn her for defiling the Teacher?

The hemorrhaging woman risked everything, reached out, and touched the Teacher's garment. As soon as she did, Jesus said, *"Someone touched me; for I noticed that power had gone out from me."* Jesus sensed power go from him because he was sensitive, not because he was in any way drained. *For in him all the fullness of God was pleased to dwell* (Colossians 1:19). There is no shortage of power in Christ. Jesus knew this woman's faith had tapped into that limitless power. What was it about her touch that made it different from the pressing of the crowd?

In the crowd that followed Jesus, most of the people pushed for a better spot. Yet Jesus discerned the difference between their touch and the woman's. "Who touched me?" he asked. Everyone denied it, although many were touching Jesus. The disciples thought Jesus' question was silly. Peter pointed out, *"Master, the crowds surround you and press in on you."* But Jesus said, *"Someone touched me; for I noticed that power had gone out from me"* (Luke 8:45-46).

Only the hemorrhaging woman touched Christ with faith, believing that his power would heal her. Her touch connected with Jesus' power. Not settling for proximity to Jesus, the hemorrhaging woman reached for Christ's power.

Today's Risk-Taking Women

Real faith involves risk. The hemorrhaging woman left the relative safety of her solitude in order to find Jesus. Most people seldom put themselves in situations that demand powerful faith. A safe, risk-free faith is more comfortable.

Think how many decisions are made on the basis of comfort alone—where, when, what we'll eat, how hard we'll work, how we'll spend a night off. Our tendency to choose the easiest path can carry over to our spiritual lives. When that happens, we stop taking risks. Even when God may want us to try something different, to change, we say no because it's too risky. It makes us uncomfortable.

When was the last time you put yourself in a position you knew you couldn't handle on your own? One woman who risked putting herself in such a position is Kathie. Kathie pressed for Christ's power to help her in her university class. "Everyone was talking about how God wasn't relevant. I sat there wishing I could be eloquent and say something intelligent to wow them. But that's not me. So I prayed and told Christ he'd have to speak through me. Finally I spoke up about my relationship with Christ. And my voice didn't even shake!" She risked speaking up and found Christ waiting to help her.

Living as a Christian should involve taking risks for God, stepping into areas where we don't feel comfortable. Through the prophets, God warned believers against becoming too comfortable.

Alas for those who are at ease in Zion, and for those who feel secure on Mount Samaria (Amos 6:1).

Elizabeth is a Christian woman who realized she was becoming too comfortable with her safe, secure life. She was grateful for all God had given her. She wanted to step out in faith and allow God's power to use her in new ways. Elizabeth began sharing her faith at work. "I know I do better behind the scenes at church and at home," she said. "But when I talk about Christ to women at work or at the store or in a dentist office, I can sense Christ working in me. I'm doing something I couldn't do on my own—God's power comes through for me!"

Zoe stepped outside of her comfortable faith when she began visiting a local nursing home. She had never felt at ease talking to strangers or being in unfamiliar situations. She felt uncomfortable around old and sick people. Zoe explains, "I went with my church to give them [nursing home residents] a Christmas party. Then I knew God wanted me to continue visiting. I go once a week, and each time I feel I just don't want to face it. But God gives me the power, and I'm always so glad I went." Zoe experiences Christ's power every time she makes a visit to the nursing home.

We each have comfort zones in faith, areas of ministering where we operate comfortably. Venturing outside those safe zones will require faith. The hemorrhaging woman was changed because she reached for Christ's power. She left the comfort of her solitary sanctuary and took a risk. We need to follow the example of our New Testament sister and stretch our faith for powerful change. Will Christ perceive power gone from him today because of our trust?

Bonding with Our Sister, the Hemorrhaging Woman

Draw a large circle on a piece of paper. Label the circle "Comfort Zone." Inside the circle, list duties, jobs, and activities you feel comfortable doing. Outside the circle, list things that represent risk-taking: talking to a friend about Christ, visiting someone in the hospital, volunteering for a duty at church, etc. Pray about doing at least one thing that lies outside your comfort zone. Do it this week. Like the hemorrhaging woman, step out in faith and keep reaching until you connect with Christ's power.

A Prayer for Other Daughters

Dear Father, thank you for the example of this bold woman who suffered so much. Thank you for loving the hemorrhaging woman and changing her life. Help me to know your love and acceptance of me as a daughter. And as a daughter, make me bold to reach out and tap into your power to change me and to touch the world around me. Amen

A Prayer to Become a Changed Woman

Thank you, Lord, for the possibility and promise of change. Help me to see myself clearly, as you see me. Help me to accept myself, but release the things you want to change in me. Make me as inquisitive as my sister, the woman of Samaria, as focused in my devotion as Mary of Bethany, and as bold as the hemorrhaging woman. Change me to be more like you. Amen

For God did not give us a spirit of
cowardice, but rather a spirit of power
and of love and of self-discipline.
(2 Timothy 1:7)

The wicked flee when no one pursues,
but the righteous are as bold as a lion.
(Proverbs 28:1)

Courageous Women

Mary Magdalene
Salome, Wife of Zebedee
Roman Women

Dear God, thank you for the courageous women I will study in this section. Help me identify with their fears and their faith. Make me bold in my beliefs and actions. Teach me to follow the examples of Mary Magdalene, Salome, and the other New Testament women who faced ridicule and danger because of their love for Christ. Give me the courage of my sisters in Christ. Amen.

Mary Magdalene

The twelve were with him, as well as some women who had been cured of evil spirits and infirmities: Mary, called Magdalene, from whom seven demons had gone out, and Joanna, the wife of Herod's steward Chuza, and Susanna, and many others, who provided for them out of their resources. (Luke 8:1-3)

Meanwhile, standing near the cross of Jesus were his mother, and his mother's sister, Mary the wife of Clopas, and Mary Magdalene. (John 19:25)

Early on the first day of the week, while it was still dark, Mary Magdalene came to the tomb and saw that the stone had been removed from the tomb. . . . But Mary stood weeping outside the tomb. As she wept, she bent over to look into the tomb. . . . Jesus said to her, "Woman, why are you weeping? Whom are you looking for?" Supposing him to be the gardener, she said to him, "Sir, if you have carried him away, tell me where you have laid him, and I will take him away." Jesus said to her, "Mary!" She turned and said to him in Hebrew, "Rabbouni!" (which means Teacher). (John 20:1, 11, 15-16)

19

∞

Courageous Love

Mary Magdalene's Courage

Mary from Magdala, a village on the western shore of the Sea of Galilee, has been the subject of dispute for centuries. Some believe Mary was the unnamed, sinful woman of Luke 7, although the Bible doesn't state the connection. Whatever the details of Mary Magdalene's life, we do know that Jesus had cast out seven demons from her. After that, this young woman was so grateful that she followed Jesus and helped with his ministry in any way she could.

Mary's life exemplifies courageous love. She stayed with Jesus at the cross, even though the twelve apostles had already fled. Mary followed Jesus' body to the tomb, then rose early to bring oil and spices to anoint his body. Peter and John left after finding the tomb empty, but Mary Magdalene stayed until she saw Jesus.

Why did Mary Magdalene act so courageously? Why did she openly identify herself with Jesus, when even Peter denied him? We may never know the full answers to those questions. Yet we can gain insight from a conversation Peter had with Jesus after Christ's resurrection. Peter had denied Christ. Yet Jesus didn't ask him, "Peter, will you be loyal?" or "Peter, will you be faithful or courageous?" Instead, Jesus asked Peter the same question three times: *"Do you love me?"* (John 21:15-19).

When Jesus was asked which commandment was the greatest, he answered, *"You shall love the Lord your God with all your heart, and with all your soul, and with all your mind"* (Matthew 22:37). Again, love was the issue. In a letter to the Corinthians, Paul wrote that out of faith, hope, and love, the greatest was love (I Corinthians 13:13).

Mary Magdalene loved Jesus. Her courage was a natural outgrowth of her love for Christ. This woman, from whom seven demons had been cast out, experienced Christ's healing and forgiveness. She knew she had been forgiven much. Jesus said, *"But the one to whom little is forgiven, loves little"* (Luke 7:47). Mary Magdalene was filled with gratitude and love, a love that produced courage.

Today's Women of Love and Courage

All of us who believe in Christ have been forgiven much. Imagine having all of our thoughts projected on a screen for everyone to view. Our thoughts and anxieties reveal how far we fall from God's perfect standard for us. When we lose sight of how much we need Christ's forgiveness, our love for Christ diminishes. Then our courage fails.

Christ wants us to admit our failings, but he doesn't want us to condemn ourselves. He wants us to accept God's forgiveness and be grateful. "Every year I love Jesus more," a woman told me on her ninetieth birthday. "I think it's because the older I get, the more clearly I see how many times I fail him and how many times he forgives."

Gratitude and love and courage are intricately connected. If we love Christ, we won't be able to sit quietly while others belittle God or other people. Our love will burn inside and make us courageous. We will speak up.

Moira is a stepmother who seeks courage in raising a difficult teenager. She explains, "When Brent acts like he hates me, I remind myself how much Christ has put up with me and how much I've been forgiven. Somehow it helps me to store up God's love; it gives me the courage to give Brent what he needs."

One day on my morning walk, I discovered that love could produce a kind of automatic courage. My three-year-old daughter,

Jenny, wandered a few paces ahead as I stopped to talk with neighbors. All of a sudden I saw a huge German shepherd racing, teeth-barred, toward my unsuspecting daughter. Before I knew what I was doing, I had beaten the dog to Jenny, grabbed her, and stuck my foot in the dog's mouth, all while three able-bodied men stood watching. I received pats on the back for my courage, but what I did was a spontaneous, instinctive act of love.

Mary Magdalene's courage stemmed from her love for Christ who had forgiven her. And Christ rewarded her love. At the Last Supper, Jesus promised to reveal himself to those who loved him. *"Those who love me will be loved by my Father, and I will love them and reveal myself to them"* (John 14:21). Mary Magdalene saw the fulfillment of that promise sooner than anyone else did. The resurrected Jesus revealed himself to her first. If we follow her example, our love will lead us to courage.

Bonding with Our Sister, Mary Magdalene

Just as Jesus forgave Mary Magdalene, he forgives us. Jesus said that the one who has been forgiven much loves much. Remind yourself how much God has forgiven you. Make a list of your actions, thoughts, attitudes, and omissions that God has forgiven. When your list is complete, write THANK YOU over it and tear it up! Now, let your love and gratitude for Christ's forgiveness move you to courageous acts of kindness and concern. Is there anything you have felt you should do but have been afraid to do (counsel a neighbor, visit someone going through a rough time, apologize, speak up, etc.)? Have the courage to follow God's leading this week.

20

⤫

Courage to Do the Next Thing

The Faithful Courage of Mary Magdalene

Jewish women in Jesus' day were expected to fulfill domestic duties, limit their public activity, and keep their heads covered. Certain aspects of the law might be taught to women so they would know what they could and could not do. But explanations of deeper theology were not discussed with "the weaker sex." Yet Jesus gathered around himself a group of women who traveled with him and supported him financially. They stayed with him at the cross and greeted him after his resurrection. Mary Magdalene is usually listed first when these women are mentioned in the Gospels.

For a woman to travel with a rabbi was not only unheard of—it was scandalous. Some of the women who followed Jesus had left their homes to be with him. Every day would have required courage as the women faced insults and disapproval.

Sometimes courage shows itself in a grand, triumphant act. More often, courage is doing what needs to be done day in and day out. Elizabeth Eliot, a missionary, author, and speaker, talks about this kind of persistent courage. She calls it "doing the next thing." Courage can mean taking advantage of what can be done, rather than allowing ourselves to be paralyzed by what can't be done. We may not understand everything that God has for us in the future, but we can always do the next thing that lies in God's will.

Mary Magdalene was courageous in doing the next thing, doing all she could do, hour by hour. Mary couldn't stop the crucifixion, but she didn't allow what she couldn't do to prevent her from doing what she could. John records, *Meanwhile, standing near the cross of Jesus were his mother, and his mother's sister, Mary the wife of Clopas, and Mary Magdalene* (John 19:25). Mary Magdalene had the courage to wait with Jesus' mother at the cross.

After the crucifixion, Mary couldn't take Christ's body home to anoint him for burial; so she did the next thing she could do. Courageously, she followed the body to the tomb. Mary couldn't embalm Jesus' body because of sabbath restrictions; so she went home and prepared spices so she would be ready to embalm the body at the earliest possible time.

Sunday morning while it was still dark, Mary Magdalene and the other women set out for the tomb. They didn't know how they would get past the Roman guards posted outside the tomb. They didn't know how they would roll away the stone that blocked the tomb's entrance. If Mary had lacked courage, she might have stayed home, overwhelmed with the impossibility of embalming Jesus' body. Instead, she did what she could. She got up early, took her prepared spices, and walked to the tomb. She did the next thing, the part of God's will that lay directly in front of her. Her courage combined with trust, and she acted. When she got to the tomb, the stone had been rolled away.

Courage often means doing the next thing we believe God wants us to do, even when we don't understand what comes after that. Psalm 119:105 says, *Your word is a lamp to my feet and a light to my path.* If the whole path is not illuminated, we can still take small steps on the part of the path that is lit. We can follow the example of Mary Magdalene and step out with courage.

Today's Courageous Women Do the Next Thing

Just as our sister Mary Magdalene courageously followed through with whatever she could do, we need to follow through with the things we can do. If we are courageous, we can always see enough of God's will to act.

Adrianna and her husband served for over forty years as British missionaries to a remote village in France. During their entire ministry, they only saw a handful of people come to Christ. When I asked Adrianna how she kept going when she saw so little come from her efforts, she answered, "I take what God's given me and offer it to one person at a time, one day at a time. Then the next day, I ask God for the courage to start fresh." Like Mary Magdalene, Adrianna found the courage to do what she could do, rather than allow herself to be paralyzed by what she could not do.

Another woman who has found a quiet, persistent courage is Jodi. Jodi is a single mom with four sons, ages six to twenty-six. She's learned the secret of doing the next thing. On days when she is overwhelmed by everything that has to be done, she looks to God for what she should do first. That question always has an answer. "I may not know what to do ten minutes from now," she says, "but I know what to do now." Jodi has the courage to act on what she knows of God's will.

Like Jodi, Marla acted on the piece of God's will she could reach. She didn't feel she could leave her school-aged children to join a world health organization, but she wanted to do something to alleviate world poverty. So, just as Mary Magdalene did so long ago, Marla did what she could. Courageously, she multiplied her own giving. She volunteered to help her church with a local food bank collection. She sponsored a child through an international children's agency. Marla found the courage to do what she could.

Mary Magdalene's courage was rewarded. She had the honor of being the first person to see the resurrected Christ. No one could receive a greater privilege. Yet Jesus gave her still more honor. *"Go to my brothers and say to them, 'I am ascending to my Father and your Father, to my God and your God'"* (John 20:17). Mary got to carry the first news of Christ's resurrection. She ran to the disciples and announced, *"I have seen the Lord."* Mary Magdalene became the first missionary—the apostle to the apostles.

Bonding with Our Sister, Mary Magdalene

Write down three things you've lacked the courage to do but you believe God wants you to do (make amends with someone, give up something, make a big change in your life—start a new job or relationship, etc.). Write down what you can do now, even though you may not know the next step. (For example, if you are considering a career move, your "next thing" may be to talk to someone in that profession.) Thank God for always revealing what we need to know about God's will and for giving us the courage to do what lies before us.

21

∞

Don't Miss the Miracle

Mary Magdalene and the Courage for Miracles

Mary Magdalene showed persistent courage and bravery inspired by love. Yet even the courageous and faithful Mary nearly missed the miracle of Christ's resurrection because she was so focused on her own plans and expectations.

All the way to the tomb, Mary and the other women worried about the big stone that had been rolled over the mouth of Jesus' grave. *They had been saying to one another, "Who will roll away the stone for us from the entrance to the tomb?"* (Mark 16:3). How would they get inside to anoint Jesus' body? Who could they get to help them push the stone away?

When the women reached the tomb, it was as if their prayers had been answered. The stone had been rolled away! As soon as Mary saw the open grave, she should have been joyful. The stone was gone! That's what she had wanted. Then she entered the tomb and found it empty. Mary should have recognized the miracle of resurrection that Christ had promised. Instead she complained, *"They have taken the Lord out of the tomb, and we do not know where they have laid him"* (John 20:2). Mary was so fixated on her own plan, she couldn't see God's greater plan for Jesus' resurrection.

Some of our richest spiritual times come when circumstances don't turn out as we expect. Mary Magdalene entered the tomb expecting to find Jesus' body. When the tomb was empty, Mary kept searching for the dead Christ. Her expectations almost made her miss the living Christ. *Supposing him to be the gardener, she said to him, "Sir, if you have carried him away, tell me where you have laid him, and I will take him away"* (John 20:15). We don't know how different Jesus may have looked. But he was standing right in front of Mary, and she didn't recognize him! It took Jesus' calling her directly to make Mary see the miracle. *"Mary!" She turned and said to him in Hebrew, "Rabbouni!"* (John 20:16).

Today's Courageous Women

God's thoughts are higher than our thoughts. Just as our sister Mary Magdalene, we may become entangled in our thoughts, and nearly miss God's thoughts. Thirteen-year-old Sally has cerebral palsy. Her mother courageously works with Sally on letters and sounds, exercises, and ordinary skills. "I used to work hard with Sally every day because I believed she would suddenly become normal. When that was my goal, I missed the everyday joys with Sally. Now I work just as hard, but I can see God's plan right here. The miracle is Sally, and I'm thankful God's given me this child."

There's a potential danger in persistent courage. While doing the next thing and taking one step at a time, as Mary Magdalene did, we may forget to look up and see God's greater plan. Elaine, an assistant manager of an expensive department store, admits it took her a year to understand God's greater plan for her life. "When I lost my job at the shoe factory, I thought it was the worst thing that could happen. I didn't realize it then, but God was teaching me to trust in him. And eventually, God had a better job waiting for me."

We may not always be able to see God's better plan as clearly as Elaine could when she got a better job. Sometimes we have to have faith that God knows what's best for us, even when we don't understand the plan. We need courage to keep looking for the miracle.

Ann decided to go to her twenty-year college reunion. "I dreaded that reunion for months, years! I'd have to face everyone as a failure. I'd started out to be a doctor, but I ended up a mom who works part time in a dentist office. On the plane ride to California, it struck me. I have a wonderful family and a rich, full life. What God has given me is great, and I hadn't been appreciating it because it didn't match this mythical forecast I'd had for myself over twenty years ago." Let's not miss the miracle in our lives, as Ann almost did.

Although Mary Magdalene is not mentioned by name in Acts, she probably was with the disciples in Jerusalem after Christ ascended to heaven. *All these* [Peter, John, James, and the other disciples] *were constantly devoting themselves to prayer, together with certain women, including Mary the mother of Jesus, as well as his brothers* (Acts 1:14).

Mary Magdalene was a faithful and courageous friend to Jesus. She may have initially missed seeing the miracle of Christ's resurrection, but she ended up embracing the miracle.

Bonding with Our Sister, Mary Magdalene

Prayerfully look back over the past few years. Can you pick out any blessings (or miracles) you failed to recognize? List several things you prayed for but didn't get. In retrospect, can you see God's grander plan for you at the time? Pray for the courage of Mary Magdalene, who in the end recognized the miracle of Christ's resurrection.

A Prayer for the Courage of Mary Magdalene

Lord, thank you for Mary Magdalene's example of courage. I confess I fall short of your standard for me. I sometimes lack in love and courage. Thank you for your forgiveness in Christ. I do love you. As Mary Magdalene did, I want to do whatever you put in front of me. Help me see your miracles. Amen.

Salome, Wife of Zebedee

Then the mother of the sons of Zebedee came to him with her sons, and kneeling before him, she asked a favor of him. And he said to her, "What do you want?" She said to him, "Declare that these two sons of mine will sit, one at your right hand and one at your left, in your kingdom." But Jesus answered, "You do not know what you are asking. Are you able to drink the cup that I am about to drink?" They said to him, "We are able." He said to them, "You will indeed drink my cup, but to sit at my right hand and at my left, this is not mine to grant, but it is for those for whom it has been prepared by my Father." (Matthew 20:20-23)

Many women were also there, looking on from a distance; they had followed Jesus from Galilee and had provided for him. Among them were Mary Magdalene, and Mary the mother of James and Joseph, and the mother of the sons of Zebedee. (Matthew 27:55-56)

When the sabbath was over, Mary Magdalene, and Mary the mother of James, and Salome bought spices, so that they might go and anoint him. And very early on the first day of the week, when the sun had risen, they went to the tomb. (Mark 16:1-2)

22

∾

Misplaced Courage

Salome's Misplaced Courage

The family of Zebedee was transformed by Jesus. Father and sons had a fishing business off the shores of the Sea of Galilee. Yet when Jesus called James and John, they left their father and the fish in the boat.

Imagine you are the mother in the Zebedee household. Yours is a fairly wealthy family, since your husband has hired men working for him. Now two of your sons—maybe that's all you have—have left the family business to follow Jesus. With your sons gone, your life has changed. Yet the change for you is just beginning. You decide to follow Jesus too!

You join the other women, such as Mary Magdalene, who follow Jesus from Galilee. From your own purse, you help provide for the needs of the disciples. Traveling with Jesus, you begin to see that your sons hold a special position with Jesus. In fact, Jesus seems to be closer to John than to anyone else. Only James, John, and Peter were allowed at the Transfiguration (Luke 9:28). Only they got to see Jesus heal Jairus' daughter (Luke 8:51).

Then Jesus begins to talk about the kingdom in heaven. One day Peter asks, *"Look, we have left everything and followed you. What then will we have?" Jesus said to them, "Truly I tell you, at the renewal of all things, when the Son of Man is seated on the throne of his glory, you who have followed me will also sit on twelve thrones, judging the twelve tribes of Israel"* (Matthew 19:27-28).

This is what you've hoped for! Your sons will rule with Jesus in this kingdom! Surely Jesus will choose your sons as second and third in command. But just in case, you decide you'll ask a little favor. You start by kneeling with James and John before Jesus. When Jesus asks what you want, you tell him: *"Declare that these two sons of mine will sit, one at your right hand and one at your left, in your kingdom"* (Matthew 20:21).

Why did Salome ask for such honor for James and John? She wanted the best for her sons, but she must have also realized the honor that would come her way as mother of the second and third in command. Salome had just heard Jesus say that he was about to be betrayed, condemned to death, mocked, flogged, and crucified (Matthew 20:18-19). Yet she chose that moment to ask for a special favor for her own sons. Pride is contagious. Salome's request came out of her pride. Her sons apparently shared that pride. When Jesus asked James and John if they were prepared to share his cup of suffering, they quickly and pridefully answered, *"We are able"* (Matthew 20:22). The other disciples had their share of pride as well. All the recorded arguments of the twelve centered around who was the greatest.

Today's Women and Misplaced Courage

Salome's request reminds me of my kids arguing before each trip: "Me first! Dibs on the front seat!" Salome wanted her kids to have front seats in the kingdom. We might see her as a silly "stage mother," pushing her children into greatness. Yet I think most of us have to identify to some degree with Salome's misplaced courage, her instinct to get what she felt was best for her sons.

We often misplace our courage. Naomi, a modern mom, thought she was helping when she asked her son's football coach to let Mike play more. The coach agreed, but Mike didn't perform well under pressure. Mike ended up feeling he wasn't good enough to be on the team. In retrospect, Naomi believes she would have been more courageous to allow Mike to develop his skills and confidence at his own pace.

Is it wrong to ask favors for our children? Not always. Sometimes we need to intervene, like the mother of a special needs child who told me, "If I didn't push teachers and principals and government officials, Joy would never get the services she's entitled to."

Do mothers know best? Sometimes, but not always. We need to consider prayerfully what we ask for ourselves and our children. Sometimes, as with Salome, we don't know what we're asking. Jesus didn't answer Salome in anger. He didn't say, "How dare you!" Instead, Jesus answered, *"You do not know what you are asking. Are you able to drink the cup that I am about to drink?"* (Matthew 20:22). Jesus knew he would be crucified. Salome didn't understand she was inviting that same treatment for her sons.

Sometimes when we get our favor granted, everything appears to have worked well, but we still may not have known best. Mary Lou couldn't stand the thought of her daughter being left out of anything. If Bree didn't get chosen for a school project, Mary Lou had the teacher add Bree to the list. She made sure Bree was invited to every party. These favors seemed to work out—until Bree got out of high school and Mary Lou could no longer orchestrate her daughter's environment. In the absence of conflict and disappointments, Bree hadn't developed the character qualities needed to deal with problems and rejections at college.

Romans 5:3-5 tells us that even in adversity we and our children can acquire wonderful qualities: perseverance, character, hope, love. What's one way we get them? *Suffering produces endurance, and endurance produces character, and character produces hope, and hope does not disappoint us.*

Hard times are opportunities to develop character. If we manipulate our way out of conflicts, we may be denying the very setting that will cause growth. Salome's misplaced courage can remind us to point our courage in the right direction. Becoming like Christ is more important than any other favor we could desire.

Bonding with Our Sister, Salome

We all want the best for ourselves and our children, just as Salome did. List character qualities you would like to see in yourself and/or in your children. Next to each quality, record at least one experience that has helped or could help you or your child develop that trait. Are you facing any problems now that might refine you and develop character? Write down each problem beside the quality that the problem might develop. Pray for the wisdom to place your courage in the right place.

23

Rebounding Courage

Salome's Rebounding Courage

Salome asked her favor—that her sons could sit at the right and left of Jesus—in front of all the disciples and probably others. We can imagine how she felt when Jesus turned her down and followed up with a sermon on true greatness. *"Whoever wishes to be first among you must be your slave"* (Matthew 20:27).

Salome must have gotten up off her knees disappointed and perhaps embarrassed. Not only had she failed to get her favor, she had shown her ignorance. She didn't understand the way Jesus' kingdom would operate. And now, because of her actions, the other ten disciples were angry with James and John.

If I had been Salome, I might have felt tempted to pack up and go back home to Zebedee, leading my sons behind me. Nobody loves criticism or rebuke, even when it's good, constructive criticism.

Yet Salome must have learned from her mistake. Instead of quitting, she followed Jesus—all the way to the cross and on to his grave (Mark 15:40, 16:1-2).

As Salome stood with Mary and watched Jesus on the cross, she might have remembered the favor she'd asked and realized it meant that James and John would share in this agony. James was in hiding. Only John was there watching with the women. From the cross, Jesus turned to his mother and to Salome's son and gave them to each other. *When Jesus saw his mother and the disciple whom he loved [John] standing beside her, he said to his mother, "Woman, here is your son." Then he said to the disciple, "Here is your mother." And from that hour the disciple took her into his own home* (John 19:26-27).

Salome's son John would be caring for Mary, who was to be his "mother." Instead of becoming a favored mother, Salome would now have to share her son. As she followed Mary to the tomb, she could have felt jealous or usurped. But Salome may have learned what it meant to be a part of Christ's kingdom. Her courage had rebounded.

Today's Women of Rebounded Courage

We are free to learn from our mistakes, as Salome apparently did, because God loves and forgives us. It is never too late to learn from mistakes. *There is therefore now no condemnation for those who are in Christ Jesus* (Romans 8:1).

In the previous chapter, we talked about conflicts and disappointments offering opportunities for us to develop in character. Making mistakes can give us the same kind of opportunity for growth. As a superintendent of city schools, Marilyn has the chance to observe teachers who rebound from their mistakes and teachers who do not. She says, "Lifelong teachers can admit mistakes, take criticism, and get on with it. They're learners." Marilyn talks sadly about other student teachers who never learned from their mistakes and continually refused to be taught. They either decided not to teach, or had short teaching careers.

Salome made a mistake by asking for her sons to be placed higher than the other disciples. When we make a mistake, we have two choices: we can learn from the mistake; or we can harden ourselves so nothing will seem to bother us. The writer of Hebrews warns believers to exhort each other *so that none of you may be hardened by the deceitfulness of sin* (3:13). If we don't admit when we've done something wrong, we will become hardened to the sin. Then if we do it again, the same mistake or sin won't seem quite so wrong. That's the "deceitfulness of sin."

Page, a junior at a state college, recognized the hardening process at work in her. "I used to think sleeping with a guy was wrong—until I did it. I felt awful the morning after. The second and third times I had sex, I didn't feel so guilty. Now the only thing I worry about is having safe sex—or getting caught by someone's wife. Sometimes I wish I could start all over. I feel like now it would be impossible to stop sleeping around."

Salome, the wife of Zebedee, is most remembered for her prideful request, just as Thomas is remembered as a doubter. Yet Salome moved beyond her mistake and grew as a disciple. There are more Salomes in the world than constantly faithful disciples. Her life gives us the confidence that we can change. We can rebound with courage just as Salome did.

Bonding with Our Sister, Salome

Salome rebounded courageously from Jesus' criticism of her mistaken request. Make a list of criticisms that have been lodged against you, both just and unjust. Next to each criticism, list anything constructive it can teach you. Finally, make a separate list of mistakes you've made but have not admitted to yourself or to God. Hand these over to God in prayer. Thank God for forgiveness in Christ. Then go on with your life in Christ as Salome did.

24

⌘

Courage to Seek God's Priorities

Salome's Godly Courage

Salome asked her favor—that her sons be second and third in command—because she misunderstood the standard operating procedures of God's kingdom. It was the custom for Oriental kings to select one person to sit at their right hand and one to sit at the left. These were the places of greatest honor.

Jesus' kingdom was different. Jesus taught, *"It will not be so among you; but whoever wishes to be great among you must be your servant, and whoever wishes to be first among you must be your slave; just as the Son of Man came not to be served but to serve, and to give his life a ransom for many"* (Matthew 20:26-28).

Salome wanted the best positions for her sons. That was natural. But very little about Jesus' kingdom is natural. It is a spiritual kingdom that demands the spiritual courage to put God's will before ours. Jesus had tried to convey how different his kingdom was from earthly kingdoms. He said the kingdom of heaven belongs to those who become like little children (Matthew 19:13-15). He explained that many who are first will be last, and the last will be first (Matthew 19:30). Pleasing God is what is important—not pleasing ourselves.

We don't have to wash our hands of everything connected with the world. We just need to put God first. *"But strive* [or, seek] *first for the kingdom of God and his righteousness, and all these things will be given to you as well"* (Matthew 6:33).

Today we have the same difficulty as our sister Salome in "putting God's kingdom first." We understand how the world around us works. We compete for position and recognition. And that's not sin in itself. Yet Jesus' kingdom operates on a different set of priorities. If someone hits you, turn the other cheek; if someone takes your suit, give him your coat too; if someone makes you go a mile, go two (Matthew 5:39-42). The "blessed" or happy people in this unnatural kingdom are the poor and hungry, those *"who are hated and excluded, reviled and defamed"* (Luke 6:20-22).

What counts isn't what other people think about the things we do. What counts is whether or not we are doing the things God wants us to do. Are God's priorities our priorities?

Today's Courageous Women of God's Kingdom

God's priorities are often radically different from the priorities we see in our world every day. Sometimes that difference makes our life a battlefield. Myra works in a bank and struggles with material and spiritual values. All day she sees people who are successful. They buy houses she would like to own. They take vacations she would like to take. In her heart, she knows her relationship with Christ is more valuable than anything else. Myra says, "Every day I have two choices. I can be jealous because they have more than I do, or be grateful because I have all I need in Christ." She seeks the courage to choose gratitude.

Nadine admits she feels drawn to two different worlds. She worked her way up in the administration of a law firm, even though she is only now finishing her college education. She explains, "I don't think God has anything against my ambition, as long as I keep offering all that I am to God first." She stays in tune with God through daily prayer and devotions. She works as hard on her spiritual growth as she does on her career.

Ramona has three children and one on the way. She admits her difficulty finding time for God. She says, "The diapers and toddlers and work around the home scream for my attention. I have to fight to think about anything else." Ramona plans times of reevaluation to adjust her priorities. About once a month, she hires a sitter and takes a planning day. She lists goals and actions and checks to make sure she is keeping Christ her first priority.

Both worlds, physical and spiritual, are real and have to be dealt with. We can't stop paying bills, quit our jobs, and ignore all material realities. But we can choose our focus, our priorities. We can make God's priorities our priorities.

We will follow Salome's example if we choose to give more of our thoughts and hearts to God's priorities than to our own.

Bonding with Our Sister, Salome

Salome learned to understand which things were God's priorities. Then she made those same things important to her. List the things that have occupied most of your thoughts today. What do your thoughts reveal about your focus? Ask God to help you focus on things that will last even after you die. List three things you want to seek (your own spiritual growth, salvation of someone you know, comfort of someone in need, justice). Like Salome, have the courage to seek God's priorities first.

A Prayer for the Courage of Salome

Lord, thank you for your honest picture of Salome, the wife of Zebedee, a woman with whom I can identify. Help me to want nothing more than to know and to serve you. Cut through my selfish desires and mold me into a courageous woman who wants what you want. Give me the courage to do what's right, what's loving, over all else. As Salome did, I want to rebound from my mistakes and grow in faith and vision. Amen.

Roman Women

Joanna
Susanna
Pilate's Wife

Soon afterwards he [Jesus] went on through cities and villages, proclaiming and bringing the good news of the kingdom of God. The twelve were with him, as well as some women who had been cured of evil spirits and infirmities: Mary, called Magdalene, from whom seven demons had gone out, and Joanna, the wife of Herod's steward Chuza, and Susanna, and many others, who provided for them out of their resources. (Luke 8:1-3)

But on the first day of the week, at early dawn, they came to the tomb, taking the spices that they had prepared. They found the stone rolled away from the tomb, but when they went in, they did not find the body. . . . Now it was Mary Magdalene, Joanna, Mary the mother of James, and the other women with them who told this to the apostles. But these words seemed to them an idle tale, and they did not believe them. (Luke 24:1-3; 10-11)

While he [Pilate] was sitting on the judgment seat, his wife sent word to him, "Have nothing to do with that innocent man, for today I have suffered a great deal because of a dream about him." (Matthew 27:19)

25

∞

Joanna, A Courageous Giver

Joanna's Giving

Before Joanna became one of Jesus' followers, she had lived in the midst of the wealth and decadence of Roman society. Her husband, Chuza, was steward to Herod Antipas, one of the sons of Herod the Great. When Herod the Great died, his three sons divided his kingdom. Herod Antipas became tetrarch of Galilee and Perea and ruled until A.D. 39. Joanna's husband managed his household and personal estate.

Chuza had to serve a suspicious, unpredictable boss in Herod Antipas. This Herod was the man Jesus called a "fox" (Luke 13:32). Herod Antipas had divorced his first wife in order to marry Herodias, his brother's wife. It was Herod Antipas who had John the Baptist beheaded. Later, he grew suspicious that Jesus might be John come back to life. Matthew records: *At that time Herod the ruler heard reports about Jesus; and he said to his servants, "This is John the Baptist; he has been raised from the dead, and for this reason these powers are at work in him"* (Matthew 14:1-2).

Joanna probably even risked her life to join the ministry of Jesus. She knew the cruelty of which Herod was capable. Yet she traveled with Jesus, a man Herod considered a threat to his kingdom. Joanna also chose to become a courageous giver, using her own resources to support the ministry. . . . *Joanna, the wife of Herod's steward Chuza . . . provided for them out of [her] resources* (Luke 8:3).

Although Joanna left her own society to join the band of Jesus' followers, she may not have been accepted immediately by those followers. Coming from the wealth of Roman privileges, she would have been an outsider.

In spite of all these obstacles, Joanna gave courageously. She gave money, but she also gave herself. Even after Christ's crucifixion, Joanna kept giving herself. She joined the women who walked to the tomb that first Easter morning. She was one of the women who told the disciples about Jesus' resurrection. Joanna's courageous giving was rewarded. Luke gives her honor with Mary Magdalene as an apostle to the apostles: *Now it was Mary Magdalene, Joanna, Mary the mother of James, and the other women with them who told this to the apostles* (Luke 24:10).

Today's Courageous Givers

Joanna might have come up with dozens of reasons for not contributing to Jesus' ministry. It was dangerous. She would offend her husband's boss and her own friends. She would have to give up her wealthy lifestyle. She wouldn't fit in with Jesus' followers. Yet she gave. Joanna's example challenges us to look past any reasons for withholding our contributions to Jesus' kingdom, and instead learn to give courageously.

We know we're supposed to support God's ministry with our resources, *for God loves a cheerful giver* (2 Corinthians 9:7). Yet most of us admit we don't give enough—enough money or enough time or enough of our talents. I asked several Christian women what kept them from giving as they felt they should.

Dana is a free-lance writer with three kids; her husband is in graduate school. She believes her lack of courageous giving was a result of misplaced priorities. She said, "I thought of my giving to church or charities as extra, as if it were not as important as the gas and electric and phone bills. I needed to make giving a priority." This year Dana has made a good first step in courageous giving. She pledged a monthly amount to her church. Then she considered it a "bill of privilege" and paid it each month before paying her other bills.

Lindsay felt she needed to give more time and money to helping other people. But as a single mom, she had to fight for time for her children. Lindsay explained, "I think the secret of courageous giving is gratitude. When I don't feel compelled to give, the problem is I'm not feeling grateful—and that's a much bigger problem. I've got to start each day telling God thank you." Recently, Lindsay and her children have gotten involved in the "Meals on Wheels" program, delivering meals to elderly people and shut-ins. They are learning the joy of giving more to each other and to other people.

Ellen had another reason for not always giving courageously. "I'm scared. I'm supporting my mother, sending my son to college, and raising a teenager, all with limited time and on a secretary's salary. I guess I'm saying I don't trust God to take care of me if I give too much. In my head, I know better, but I'm scared." Ellen has started spending more time in prayer and Bible study. As she gets to know God better, she feels she can trust God more. Then she gains the courage to give.

God promises that when we risk in our giving as Joanna did, we will not be left empty. *Give, and it will be given to you. A good measure, pressed down, shaken together, running over, will be put into your lap; for the measure you give will be the measure you get back* (Luke 6:38).

Bonding with Our Sister, Joanna

Joanna felt compelled to follow Jesus and give all she could to his ministry. This week, consider the needs of another person. Do you know someone who is going through a hard time? Are you aware of a financial need? Give as God leads you to give—in time and/or in money. Pay a visit, or pay a bill. Ask God to show you one thing you can do to help meet another person's need. Try to be as courageous in your giving as Joanna.

26

~

Susanna, A Quiet Giver

Susanna's Giving

The twelve were with him, as well as some women who had been cured of evil spirits and infirmities: Mary, called Magdalene, from whom seven demons had gone out, and Joanna, the wife of Herod's steward Chuza, and Susanna, and many others, who provided for them out of their resources (Luke 8:1-3).

Susanna is one of those women mentioned in Scripture about whom we wish we knew more. Although most women in the New Testament are identified by their relationships to their husbands or sons (Joanna, wife of Chuza; Mary, John Mark's mother; Pilate's wife; Mary, mother of James and Joses; Salome, wife of Zebedee and mother of James and John), Susanna's name stands on its own. We know only a few facts about Susanna. She was a Roman woman (Susanna was a Roman name). She was healed by Jesus (*some women who had been cured of evil spirits and infirmities*). And she gave generously to Jesus and the ministry (she's included as one of the women *who provided for [the disciples] out of their resources*).

Although wealthy, upper-class, Roman women in Jesus' day had more freedom in society than Jewish women in Galilee, the Roman Empire still considered women second-class citizens. Susanna probably had no real decision-making authority in her society. We don't know what she had to give up to follow Jesus.

Susanna's giving did not seem to bring her fame in her day or in ours. She is not as well-known as Mary Magdalene or some of the other New Testament women. Susanna simply did her part like many women before her and many women since.

Susanna is part of a long, rich heritage of giving women. The Widow of Zarephath, for example, used her last oil and grain to make bread for the prophet Elijah (I Kings 17:8-24). The Shunammite woman built on a little room to keep ready for Elisha, Elijah's successor (2 Kings 4:8-10). A certain poor widow was observed by Jesus and his disciples at the temple in Jerusalem. She put in an offering of two small copper coins worth a penny. Jesus praised her for putting in everything she had to live on (Mark 12:41-44). All of these women gave whatever they could courageously—food, shelter, or coins. They made what they did possess available for God's work.

Luke 8:3 says Susanna and Joanna and other women *provided for* Jesus and the disciples. The Greek word *diakoneo*, translated *provided for*, describes the kind of generous giving these women did. The word means to serve, wait on, or minister to as deacon. In the early Christian community, *diakoneo* included not only domestic chores but also proclamation of the word and eucharistic table service.

Today's Giving Women

Just as our sister Susanna gave quietly and perhaps without notice, women today often give without receiving great recognition. They give generously and courageously because God has given to them.

Esther is a modern example of giving quietly, without fanfare. Esther has been a faithful volunteer at her church for over thirty years. Yet few people realize what she has contributed, and no one compliments her for a job well done. Still, every Friday night and Saturday this giving woman carefully folds bulletins with arthritic hands. Esther says she prefers to do her part quietly so she will know her labor is for God and not for personal recognition.

Meredith, an attorney, gives in a way that reminds us of the Shunammite woman who kept a room ready for Elisha. Meredith regularly invites women to her house for dinner or an evening of board games. She tries to ask women who may not get invited out often. She explains that she is not a natural hostess. "I enjoy people, but I'm basically a hermit at heart. Still, I know God wants me to give myself this way." Only people who are close to Meredith realize how fully she has to rely on God for the courage to be hostess.

Charise comes from a family of successful people. Her brother has achieved a certain fame as a writer, her sister is a doctor, and her parents were fairly well-known in political circles. Instead of pursuing college and a career for herself, however, Charise chose to stay home and take care of her father after he suffered a stroke. She is still caring for her father, and she says she doesn't resent her lack of education or fame. Instead she is grateful to God. Charise is a quiet giver.

Christ's unrestrained love for us compels us to give to others. Just as Susanna ministered as she could, quietly for God, we can let God use us to give ourselves in any way we can.

Bonding with Our Sister, Susanna

Susanna gave quietly and courageously. Consider some things God might want you to give (time, talent, possessions, money). Plan to follow through on at least one of these gifts before the week is out.

27

∞

Pilate's Wife Speaks Up

Pilate's Wife Risks Speaking Up

When Jesus was arrested in the Garden of Gethsemane, he suffered many kinds of betrayal. Judas, one of his twelve disciples, had betrayed him with a kiss. Soldiers armed with swords and clubs took him into custody. No one spoke up in his defense. Instead, his disciples ran away.

Next Jesus was taken to stand before the Jewish high priest and Jewish council. Witnesses testified against him. Once again, no one spoke in his defense. While Jesus was being questioned, mocked, and beaten by guards, Peter was down in the temple courtyard denying any association with him.

Pilate sent Jesus to King Herod, who was also in Jerusalem at that time. During Jesus' trial with Herod, soldiers beat and mocked Jesus. Again, no one spoke up for him or tried to stop the proceedings.

Herod returned Jesus to Pontius Pilate, governor of Judea, who sentenced Jesus to death by crucifixion. Jesus had been betrayed by Judas, denied by Peter, and deserted by his disciples. Only one person spoke up to stop Pilate's verdict—the wife of Pontius Pilate.

Pilate conducted his interviews with Jesus and found nothing that merited a death sentence. Yet he was under pressure from Rome and from the crowds in Jerusalem. As governor of Judea, Pilate's job was to keep the peace in his province. So far, he was not succeeding.

His cruelties had led to riots and insurrections. Pilate had been warned by Rome to work with Jewish authorities for a peaceful coexistence. So Pilate decided to sentence Jesus to death.

Then something happened to make Pilate think again. As he sat on his judgment seat, Pilate received a message . . . from his wife: *"Have nothing to do with that innocent man, for today I have suffered a great deal because of a dream about him"* (Matthew 27:19).

There is much we don't know about this story. Had Pilate and his wife discussed Jesus before? She certainly knew about the trial and what rested on its outcome. How well did she know Jesus? She was convinced of his innocence. God selected this courageous woman to receive a dream, and she understood it.

Tradition identifies Pilate's wife as Claudia Procula. She probably spent most of her time in the Judean town of Caesarea along the Mediterranean Sea, where Pilate had his headquarters. Many speculative stories were told about Claudia Procula by later Christians. Some said she was a Jewish proselyte and secret follower of Jesus. Others claimed she was the Claudia mentioned by the apostle Paul in 2 Timothy 4:21.

What we do know for certain is that this woman followed an internal insight to warn her husband that Jesus was innocent. She was courageous. She dared to speak up.

Pilate's wife ran a risk of reprisal by sending Pilate a warning. Her husband was a volatile man, and she carried no authority. She dared to call Jesus an "innocent man" before Pilate passed judgment on him. Pilate was sitting on the judgment seat, surrounded by other people. She was interrupting important business. Maybe he would appear weak by listening to his wife. Yet in spite of everything, she spoke up.

Today's Women Speak Up

All of us at one time or another, like Pilate's wife, have opportunities to speak up when we see or hear of injustices. We may see someone being taken advantage of, or ridiculed, or perhaps simply ignored when in need of help. Perhaps we know someone who needs to hear about Christ, but we're afraid to say anything. Marissa recognized such an opportunity and responded to it. When Marissa's family learned about her brother David's affair, only Marissa dared to confront him. She explains, "I don't know if it helped or not, but I'm convinced it was my responsibility to speak up."

On the other hand, Jan laments a time when she didn't speak up. "Carol and I knew Diane drank too much. We talked about it with each other, but not with her. One night, after too much to drink, Diane drove head on into a pole and was killed. I don't know if warning her would have done Diane any good, but I should have said something at the very least."

Sometimes our warnings are ignored, but we still should speak up. We don't know what became of Pilate's wife. She might have felt like a failure as Jesus was led away to be crucified. Perhaps she mourned him and wondered why she had been given a dream to save an innocent man who was killed anyway. Still, she had spoken up courageously. She had done what she could.

Isaiah promises that a word from God *shall not return to me empty, but it shall accomplish that which I purpose, and succeed in the thing for which I sent it* (Isaiah 55:11). Although Pilate may not have learned from his wife's warning, we can. Her example of speaking up courageously can compel us to listen for what God tells us to say, and then say it!

Bonding with Our Sister, Pilate's Wife

Pilate's wife might have kept quiet, but instead she risked speaking up for Christ, a stranger in trouble. Think of the last time you failed to speak up when you knew you should. It may have been with your family. It may have been an opportunity to defend someone. What was the real reason you didn't speak up (fear of failure, fear of what people might think, apathy)? Now, imagine a similar situation that could happen this week. Write down what you should say. Check your motive for speaking up. Be ready to say what you need to say. As Pilate's wife was, be courageous in speaking up.

A Prayer for Giving Ourselves

Lord, I feel I have much in common with the first century women of Rome—Joanna, Susanna, and Pilate's wife. My world is filled with wealth and luxury and possessions that tempt me. Help me listen to you and value my relationship with you more than any other thing. Help me to be a courageous giver. Make me like Joanna and Susanna, willing to risk condemnation because I am giving to God's ministry. Make me bold to speak up as Pilate's wife was courageous in speaking up for Christ. Thank you for these women, my kindred sisters in Christ. Amen.

A Prayer to Become a Courageous Woman

Thank you God for the examples of the courageous women. Help me to speak up as Pilate's wife did. Make me bold in defending others and standing up for what I know is right. Help me be a giver, like Joanna and Susanna. I want to follow you courageously as my sisters Mary Magdalene and Salome did. Grant to me their courage to do the piece of your will you set in front of me. Make me a woman of courage day after day. Amen.

Whatever your task, put yourselves
into it, as done for the Lord
and not for your masters.
(Colossians 3:23)

"If you know these things, you are
blessed if you do them."
(John 13:17)

Enterprising Women

Lydia
Priscilla
Women Who Were Doers

Lord, thank you for the examples you have given me in the enterprising women of the New Testament. Help me cross time and culture to identify with their struggles. Like them, I want to use my talents, my resources, and my opportunities to help others and to spread your good news everywhere. Make me as bold and independent as Lydia, the businesswomen. Make me willing to be a team player like Priscilla. Help me use my special enterprising abilities in unique ways, as Tabitha, Lois, Eunice, and Rufus' mother did. Amen.

Lydia

On the sabbath day we went outside the gate by the river, where we supposed there was a place of prayer; and we sat down and spoke to the women who had gathered there. A certain woman named Lydia, a worshiper of God, was listening to us; she was from the city of Thyatira and a dealer in purple cloth. The Lord opened her heart to listen eagerly to what was said by Paul. When she and her household were baptized, she urged us, saying, "If you have judged me to be faithful to the Lord, come and stay at my home." And she prevailed upon us. (Acts 16:13-15)

After leaving the prison they [Paul and Silas] went to Lydia's home; and when they had seen and encouraged the brothers and sisters there, they departed. (Acts 16:40)

28

❦

The Right Risk

Lydia's Enterprise

Lydia originally came from Thyatira, a city in Lydia (a province in present-day Turkey). The province of Lydia was known for its purple dye. Lydians were the first to devise a coin medium of standard exchange, and inscriptions discovered in ruins suggest Thyatira spawned more trade guilds than any other city of its day. Lydia grew up in a world of business and commerce.

Lydia may have belonged to the Guild of Purple-Sellers, famed throughout the Roman Empire for royal garments. Purple dye came from two sources around Thyatira: the madder root and a rare kind of shell fish. The veins of the shell fish, when exposed to the sun, produced one tiny drop of purple dye per fish. The process rendered purple dye for garments extremely expensive.

Lydia is called a seller of purple garments—the same type of robes used to mock Christ: *And the soldiers wove a crown of thorns and put it on his head, and they dressed him in a purple robe. They kept coming up to him saying, "Hail, King of the Jews!"* (John 19:2-3).

Religion and business were integrally linked in Thyatira. The city's legendary hero was Tyrimnos. He was thought to be a divine ancestor of the town's leading families, for whom he acted as a protecting god. Coins carried the image of Tyrimnos.

Lydia was a Gentile who might have found a prominent position in Thyatiran religious life. Instead, she chose to worship the Jewish God. Lydia had become a proselyte, a "worshiper of God" (Acts 16:14). Following Judaism set her apart from the people who were probably her best customers. Lydia risked losing business because of her faith.

At some point, Lydia moved 250 miles to Philippi, a Roman outpost in what is northern Greece today. Here, on the banks of a river outside the city gates, Lydia met Paul and came to a faith in Christ. She and all her household were baptized. Although some of Lydia's female relatives may have been included, it's more likely that her "household" refers to other people involved in her business. Stores in first-century Macedonia generally had a business on the ground floor, with living quarters on the second floor.

Outside the gates to the city, an inscription prohibited the entrance of any new religion. Lydia had risked losing Gentile customers when she became a Jewish God-fearer. Now she took another risk. Lydia was baptized and identified herself with Christ and his followers. She also risked losing her Jewish customers.

Lydia refused to allow her business enterprise to limit her faith. She embraced the new religion. And the Philippian church that grew out of her home served the early Christian movement well. The Philippians were the only ones who consistently sent Paul money to support his work. Most letters Paul wrote to the other early churches were sent to correct them or to keep them on the right track. Paul's letter to the Philippians is a thank-you note!

Today's Enterprising Women Combine Faith and Business

Like Lydia, many women today face alienation when they combine faith and business. One example is Justina, who works in a downtown office building. She admits she is tempted to stifle her faith when she's on the job. Justina says, "When God does something great in my life or I feel especially close to the Lord, I share it at church but never at work. But I want to change. I want to be the same person at both places."

Patricia is a pastor, and even she has trouble keeping "business" and faith unified. "There's a lot of business to running a church," she says. "Sometimes, I forget that faith and guidance from the Spirit have to be part of every decision. Often I'd rather just get the business part done myself."

Vicki and her husband run a large dairy in central Ohio. The first thing customers see when they enter the dairy is a sign that reads: THIS DAIRY IS RUN TO THE GLORY OF GOD THE FATHER AND GOD'S SON, JESUS CHRIST. LIKE THE THREE-LEGGED DAIRY STOOL, WE ARE SUPPORTED BY THE FATHER, SON, AND HOLY SPIRIT. Vicki says she knows they have lost a few customers "who didn't think we should get our religion mixed up in our milking." But she's not about to take the sign down. She's made her business and her faith part of the same world.

Lydia shows us how much a business woman can affect her world when her business is one with her faith. If we follow Lydia's example of enterprising faith, we can change our world, too.

Bonding with Our Sister, Lydia

Lydia was faithful in her business enterprise. List the work that takes up most of your day. Now list any restraints on expressing your faith you have felt in your work environment. Could you lose your job or your customers as Lydia did? Prayerfully go over your list and circle any fears that are not really business fears ("People will think I'm funny if I read the Bible at work." "Talking about Christ will label me a quack." "Sticking up for someone will make me unpopular.") Choose several items from your list and target them this week. Make an effort to express your faith in those specific situations.

29

∞

The Right Place

Lydia's Journey to the Right Place

Lydia moved from her home in Thyatira (now western Turkey) to Philippi in Macedonia (present-day Greece). Philippi was an excellent place for news to spread to Asia and Europe. From this busy Roman outpost, the word of Christ could spread in every direction.

For Lydia too, Philippi was the right place. There she met the apostle Paul. *On the sabbath day we went outside the gate by the river, where we supposed there was a place of prayer; and we sat down and spoke to the women who had gathered there* (Acts 16:13).

Because the Jews had no synagogue inside the city, Lydia and others gathered faithfully outside the city gate. Generally, a city with as many as ten Jewish males could form its own synagogue. Philippi may not have had ten Jewish males, or the city may have enforced its ban on new religions. Lydia was enterprising in her faith as well as in her business. She met for worship by the riverside according to Jewish custom dating back hundreds of years. Lydia's faithfulness put her in the right place to hear the word of Christ.

Lydia believed the gospel and opened her home to Paul and his companions. Paul and Silas were staying with Lydia when they were arrested and thrown into prison. When the men were released from prison, they went directly to Lydia's home. Luke tells us what they found at Lydia's. *After leaving the prison they went to Lydia's home; and when they had seen and encouraged the brothers and sisters there, they departed* (Acts 16:40). There were other brothers and sisters meeting there! The Philippian church was beginning in Lydia's home.

Lydia was an enterprising woman who followed God's leadership. Her obedience led her to the right place where God could meet her and use her in a powerful way.

Today's Enterprising Women

As Lydia followed God's leading to the "right place," enterprising women today want to follow God to their own "right places." Maria works with the Red Cross in Pennsylvania. She knows God has brought her to the right place. All she did was follow. She says, "Ten years ago, I could never have told you this is where I should be or what I should be doing. I just took the little steps along the way and knew they were right. I volunteered to help at a youth camp. Then I worked at a halfway house, then with the Red Cross. Each step brought me closer to where I am now." Lydia and Maria ended up in the right place because they followed God.

Sometimes we may be in the "right place," but we just don't realize it. Then something seemingly insignificant happens and we understand. We grasp the fact that we are exactly where we should be. I call these times of insight "right moments." Many women have experienced them.

Danita experienced a "right moment" at her daughter's sixth-grade basketball game, "the most boring sporting event in the world." She explained, "I was churning inside because I had a thousand other things I could have been doing. Then I prayed, and I felt this relaxed peace because I knew I was exactly where I was supposed to be. Nothing earth-shattering happened. My daughter's team lost; she didn't act grateful for my presence. But God's Spirit in my heart gave me the assurance that I was where God wanted me to be at that moment. Everything else would have to get by without me."

Lydia traveled a distance and risked business losses to follow God's leading. Her steps of faith led her to Philippi the day Paul came to preach the gospel. If we follow the example of our enterprising sister Lydia, we can know that we will end up in the place God wants us to be.

Bonding with Our Sister, Lydia

Lydia may have wondered at times whether moving to Philippi was the right step for her. Do you ever wonder if you are in the right place? What reasons convince you that you are in the right place at the right time now (moments of inner confirmation? prayerful decisions made in the past, etc.)? Ask God to show you any right places and any wrong places in your life. Thank God for all the "rights" in your life, and ask God for help in changing direction when you need to.

30

The Right Heart

Lydia's Heart Opens

Every sabbath Lydia met for prayer with a group of women out-side the gates of Philippi. When Paul stopped at the riverside, Lydia's heart was prepared to listen to him. And the Holy Spirit opened her heart to respond to the word of Jesus Christ. *A certain woman named Lydia, a worshiper of God, was listening to us. . . . The Lord opened her heart to listen eagerly to what was said by Paul* (Acts 16:14). What does it mean for Lydia to have God "open her heart"?

The metaphor of God opening hearts is used elsewhere in Scripture. Although several words for open appear in the New Tes-tament, Acts uses the Greek word *dianoigo* (to open up completely) to describe what the Lord did to Lydia's heart. God radically inter-vened to make Lydia more receptive to the word of Christ. God opened her heart completely to help her understand.

A similar "heart opening" had occurred earlier on the road to Emmaus. The resurrected Christ appeared to two of his followers, but they didn't recognize him. Jesus called them *"slow of heart to believe all that the prophets have declared."* He interpreted the scriptures for them and broke bread with them. *Then their eyes were opened [dianoigo], and they recognized him . . . . They said to each other, "Were not our hearts burning within us while he was talking to us on the road, while he was opening the scriptures to us?"* (Luke 24:25, 31-32).

On the road to Emmaus and on the riverside of Philippi, God opened hearts through the instrument of the word, called the sword in Ephesians. *Take the helmet of salvation, and the sword of the Spirit, which is the word of God* (Ephesians 6:17).

Indeed, the word of God is living and active, sharper than any two-edged sword. . . . it is able to judge the thoughts and intentions of the heart (Hebrews 4:12). Here is more evidence that the sharp tool for opening the heart is the word of God.

The word of God preached by Paul opened Lydia's heart. She in turn opened her home to the disciples and urged them until they agreed to stay with her. She spoke out and passed God's word on to others. When she encountered new believers, she opened her home to them, and a church grew out of her home.

The entire Philippian church was based on the generosity of women like Mary Magdalene, Joanna, and Susanna. At least four times the Philippians sent gifts to other churches—to Thessalonica, to Corinth, and to Rome. Our sister Lydia leaves us an example of enterprising generosity with worldwide repercussions.

Today's Open-Hearted Women

Like Lydia, women today are still having their hearts opened by God. In response, women are opening their hearts to others. Kim is a widow who became a Christian when a friend shared the Bible with her many years ago. Ever since then, she has been opening her heart to others. Kim works as a volunteer for soup kitchens, fund drives, meals-on-wheels, and half a dozen other charitable organizations. She sees a direct correlation between the work God did in her heart when she became a Christian and the work she now does in her community.

As a teenager, Juanita responded to the Bible when a friend dragged her to church. "The pastor quoted Ephesians 2:8-9, which says that salvation is by faith, not works. That night I understood how to accept Christ's gift. Ever since then, I have tried to give to others."

Like Juanita, Bethany believes God opened her heart. Unlike Juanita, Bethany was already a believer. She had been an active church member for years when God used a passage in Scripture to show her something about herself. She explained, "I was preparing to teach a Sunday school lesson but learned something myself when I hit a verse in Romans 2 that says we should not judge other people. I had been so down on my sister because she refused to teach a Bible class or help out at church. But as soon as I read the Romans verse about not judging, I could feel in my heart how wrong I was." God opened Bethany's heart so that she could see herself more clearly.

When God opens our hearts and we respond, our lives show the change. Lydia's open heart resulted in a series of openings as she opened her own home to other believers. We can follow Lydia's example and listen eagerly to words about Christ. This allows God to open our hearts. In turn, we can open ourselves to others.

Bonding with Our Sister, Lydia

As Lydia listened to the word of Christ, God opened her heart. Think back over your life as a believer. Make a list of verses from the Bible that God has used to show you something about yourself or your attitude. Write them down. Beside each verse, record the lesson God taught you. This week, try setting aside at least fifteen minutes every day to read from the New Testament. Pray that God will open your heart more fully. Then record what God shows you and how your heart changes. How will you in turn open your heart to someone else in the coming week?

A Prayer for Open-Hearted Enterprise

Lord, I want to follow you wholeheartedly as my sister Lydia did. Open my heart to understand what you have to say to me. Help me use my enterprises to do your work on earth. Make me like Lydia, brave enough to risk loss of business or prestige if it means completing your business here. Make me able and willing. Amen.

Priscilla

After this Paul left Athens and went to Corinth. There he found a Jew named Aquila, a native of Pontus, who had recently come from Italy with his wife Priscilla, because Claudius had ordered all Jews to leave Rome. Paul went to see them, and, because he was of the same trade, he stayed with them, and they worked together—by trade they were tentmakers. (Acts 18:1-3)

After staying there for a considerable time, Paul said farewell to the believers and sailed for Syria, accompanied by Priscilla and Aquila. . . . When they reached Ephesus, he left them there. (Acts 18:18-19)

He [Apollos] began to speak boldly in the synagogue; but when Priscilla and Aquila heard him, they took him aside and explained the Way of God to him more accurately. (Acts 18:26)

Greet Prisca [alternate form of Priscilla] and Aquila, who work with me in Christ Jesus, and who risked their necks for my life, to whom not only I give thanks, but also all the churches of the Gentiles. (Romans 16:3-4)

The churches of Asia send greetings. Aquila and Prisca, together with the church in their house, greet you warmly in the Lord. (I Corinthians 16:19)

31

❦

Priscilla the Itinerant Minister

Priscilla on the Move

Priscilla and her husband, Aquila, were Jewish tentmakers living in Rome during the turbulent reign of Claudius. The Emperor, fed up with riots and disputes among the Jews in his country, issued an edict in A.D. 49 expelling all Jews from Rome. This expulsion marked the beginning of a plan of itinerant ministry God had for Priscilla and her husband.

Priscilla and Aquila had started a business enterprise in a country where Roman citizens looked down on Jews, and Jews despised Christians. They worked to build their enterprise and home in Rome. Then one day they were expelled. They would have to begin all over again.

From Rome, Priscilla and Aquila moved to Corinth. Corinth was a melting pot of religions and a city full of wealth and immorality. As a strategic seaport and the capital of Achaia (present day Greece), Corinth earned its reputation as the most decadent city in the world. Over a dozen pagan temples operated throughout the city. The Temple of Aphrodite boasted 1,000 prostitutes. Other cities in the Roman Empire referred to prostitutes as "Corinthian girls." If someone called you Corinthian, it meant you were immoral. This was the world that surrounded Priscilla and her husband as they built up their tentmaking enterprise.

Corinth is where Priscilla and Aquila met Paul. *After this Paul left Athens and went to Corinth. There he found a Jew named Aquila, a native of Pontus, who had recently come from Italy with his wife Priscilla, because Claudius had ordered all Jews to leave Rome. Paul went to see them, and, because he was of the same trade, he stayed with them, and they worked together—by trade they were tentmakers* (Acts 18:1-3). Imagine what work on the tents may have been like as Priscilla labored in the commercial enterprise with Paul and Aquila! Then she labored with them in spiritual enterprise.

When Paul left Corinth, Priscilla and Aquila went with him. Again they left their customers and the business they had built up. This time, they traveled to Ephesus, a banking center and one of the chief cities of the ancient world. As in Corinth, Priscilla and her husband met with religious opposition. The Ephesians worshiped the mother goddess Artemis, and idols of this many-breasted goddess of fertility were sold by silversmiths all over Ephesus. Silversmiths like Demetrius saw this new religion of Christianity as a threat to their trade. They incited the crowds to riot against Paul.

Paul left Ephesus for Jerusalem. Priscilla and Aquila stayed to build up the church in Ephesus. Priscilla knew how to bloom where she was planted. She made a home, a business, and a ministry wherever God led her. Her enterprising faith made her an effective itinerant minister.

At some point Priscilla and Aquila must have moved back to Rome. When Paul closed his letter to the Romans, he sent greetings to the couple and added, *Greet also the church in their house* (Romans 16:5). Once more, Priscilla had been able to minister in a new place. Her home was more than the particular city where she resided. Priscilla's home was in Christ. The security of that home freed her to minister wherever she went.

Philippians 3:20 says, *But our citizenship is in heaven.* Our real home is with Christ. That security, however, should never make us feel that what we do on earth is unimportant. On the contrary, knowing that we have a home in heaven should free us to serve as itinerant ministers on earth, just as Priscilla did. When our own children feel they have a safe, happy home to return to, they are more free to explore the world outside. In the same way, we are free to go wherever God sends us because we know where our eternal home is.

Today's Women as Itinerant Ministers

In the first century, leaving a home country uprooted a person's life. Modern Americans are more mobile. We move from state to state, job to job. But even today, change can shake us to the core. It takes a secure faith to start over.

Shana moved to France in order to keep her job as an entertainment promoter. She explains the spiritual struggle that followed. "I kept thinking, this does not feel like home. I was so wrapped up in trying to feel at home, I never even thought about what opportunities I might find to minister to others. After a few weeks I found several Christians who met for prayer. With them, I felt at home. It reminded me where my home really was. I began to look around to see how God could use me in France. Almost immediately I met two women at work who were very interested in learning more about Christ."

Perhaps Priscilla could let herself be uprooted so easily because her roots had sunk deep into Christ rather than into her surroundings. Her home was in heaven. Her treasure and her heart were there also. Priscilla used her earthly homes in Corinth, Ephesus, and Rome to serve others and to minister on earth.

Bonding with Our Sister, Priscilla

Priscilla had an enterprising faith. As clearly as you can, define the ministry or ministries God has given you where you live (home, neighborhood, work, extended family, friends). How can the security of a home in heaven free you to act for Christ on earth? What can you do to expand the ministries God has given you?

32

❧

Priscilla, A Team Player

Priscilla's Team

Priscilla's name appears with her husband's every time she is mentioned in the New Testament. But if our picture of the ideal Christian couple is one where the husband ministers and the wife quietly supports him at home, then Priscilla and Aquila don't fit the model. In New Testament times it was customary to list the most important person's name first, to place the husband's name before his wife's. However, Priscilla's name comes before Aquila's in four of the six times they appear. Luke calls both of them tentmakers—*by trade they were tentmakers* (Acts 18:3). Paul left both of them in charge of the church at Ephesus. Both Priscilla and Aquila took Apollos, an itinerant minister from Alexandria, into their home in order to teach him the complete message of Christ.

Priscilla and Aquila were a valuable team. We get a picture of how valuable Paul considered Priscilla and her husband in the greetings he sent in a letter to the Corinthian church. *The churches of Asia send greetings. Aquila and Prisca* [alternate form of Priscilla], *together with the church in their house, greet you warmly in the Lord* (1 Corinthians 16:19). In his last letter to Timothy, Paul wrote, *Greet Prisca and Aquila, and the household of Onesiphorus* (2 Timothy 4:19).

Finally, Paul praised Priscilla and Aquila when he wrote to the Romans, *Greet Prisca and Aquila, who work with me in Christ Jesus, and who risked their necks for my life, to whom not only I give thanks, but also all the churches of the Gentiles* (Romans 16:3).

Priscilla and Aquila were encouragers. First they ministered to Paul when he came to Corinth. Paul arrived in Corinth discouraged from his time in Athens. He described himself as *afflicted in every way—disputes without and fears within* (2 Corinthians 7:5). In his first letter to the Corinthians Paul reminisced: *And I came to you in weakness and in fear and in much trembling* (2:3). Then he met the tentmakers, Priscilla and Aquila. They welcomed Paul, and the three of them became an effective team.

When Paul left Corinth for Syria, he took Priscilla and Aquila with him. Paul went on to Jerusalem, but he left Priscilla and Aquila in Ephesus. He knew he could count on them to continue his ministry.

While Priscilla and Aquila were in Ephesus, a Jew named Apollos arrived in the city. He was intelligent and eloquent. He had been educated in Alexandria, the center of philosophy and home of the largest library in the world at that time. As Priscilla listened to Apollos in the synagogue, she realized that he spoke with enthusiasm about the "Way of the Lord." Apollos only knew the things concerning Jesus up to his baptism by John. He apparently didn't know about the significance of the resurrection or Pentecost.

Priscilla and Aquila could have felt jealous of Apollos' eloquence. They might have challenged him in the synagogue, or compromised their beliefs and left Apollos on his own. Instead, *when Priscilla and Aquila heard him, they took him aside and explained the Way of God to him more accurately* (Acts 18:26). Priscilla recognized they were all on the same team in the enterprise of faith.

Apollos accepted instruction in the same spirit it was given. Priscilla and Aquila and the believers at Ephesus encouraged Apollos and sent along a letter of recommendation when he wanted to move on. Apollos proved to be a powerful member of the team. Paul wrote to Corinth, *I planted, Apollos watered, but God gave the growth* (I Corinthians 3:6).

Priscilla was a team player. She lived out the advice Paul gave Timothy: *And the Lord's servant must not be quarrelsome but kindly to everyone, an apt teacher, patient, correcting opponents with gentleness* (2 Timothy 2:24-25).

Today's Team Players

What does it mean to serve Christ as a couple, as Priscilla and Aquila did? As individual believers, we minister in many ways. *There are varieties of services, but the same Lord* (I Corinthians 12.5-6). As couples, our teamwork expresses itself differently. We need to be careful not to limit ourselves or our sisters in Christ to our version of the ideal Christian couple.

Teams operate in different ways. Fran and Tanya are married to pastors. Fran works behind the scenes, doing everything she can to free up her husband so he will have more time for his congregation. She's happy with the role she's chosen because she knows her husband's ministry is hers, too. Tanya, on the other hand, is less involved in church. She feels God has given her a different avenue of ministry. She teaches aerobics and uses her classes as a means to share Christ with women in the community. Tanya feels she and her husband minister together as a different kind of team.

Olivia is single, yet she has found a team in her neighbors. She explains, "The young couple next door could be my son and daughter. We're that close. We started out working together as a neighborhood watch for safety, but we've become a neighborhood care group."

Priscilla knew how to be a team player—with her husband, with Paul, with Apollos, and with believers in the cities where she lived. If we follow her example, we can increase our effectiveness in ministry and in enterprise.

Bonding with Our Sister, Priscilla

Priscilla worked as a team member in several different situations. Define any teams you are a part of (family, church committee, sports, job). How do you already serve Christ on your teams? What three problems do you run up against most often on any team? Write down a change you can make in attitude or action for the sake of your team. Just as Priscilla did, be an enterprising woman who knows how to work with others as a teammate.

33

∞

Priscilla, A Marathoner

Priscilla's Endurance

Priscilla is one of the few New Testament women we get to observe repeatedly over a number of years. First, she and her husband, Aquila, were expelled from Italy. When we meet her in Acts 18 in Corinth, Priscilla is welcoming Paul into her home and making tents with the men. A year and a half to two years later Priscilla boarded a boat to Ephesus, where she and her husband started one of the most influential churches of the first century. Years later Paul sent greetings to Priscilla, her husband, and the church that met in their house.

At the end of his life, Paul stopped in Ephesus to say good-bye. Priscilla was probably there when Paul gave a final encouragement: *"I do not count my life of any value to myself, if only I may finish my course and the ministry that I received from the Lord Jesus, to testify to the good news of God's grace"* (Acts 20:24). Later Paul wrote Timothy, *I have fought the good fight, I have finished the race, I have kept the faith* (2 Timothy 4.7).

Priscilla could have said the same thing. She fought the good fight. Most of us have known people who seemed to have a growing faith in Christ but then somehow lose their zeal. It is as if they have dropped out of the race. Part of being enterprising in our faith is sticking with it to the end, as Priscilla did.

Why do some believers fail to go the distance with their faith? One reason we stop growing in and practicing our Christian faith is fear. Priscilla faced genuine physical threats in the first century. In a letter, Paul told the Romans that more than once Priscilla and Aquila *risked their necks for my life* (Romans 16:3). He may have been alluding to the Roman practice of the day—beheading for crimes against the state. We may not face physical dangers, but other fears can obstruct our growth in Christ and keep us from being enterprising in our faith.

Today's Faithful, Enterprising Women

Ashley describes a kind of fear that could have short-circuited her faith. A decade ago she helped bring government financed housing into her community because she wanted to help homeless women and children. Many of Ashley's neighbors did not appreciate the change in their neighborhood. Ashley has continued her work, finding jobs for the jobless. And she has worked to help promote harmony among her old and new neighbors.

Our enterprising and enduring faith can be obstructed by fear, or we may just run out of steam a little at a time. Paul wrote to encourage the Corinthians to be like athletes who train every day. *Athletes exercise self-control in all things; they do it to receive a perishable wreath, but we an imperishable one* (1 Corinthians 9:25).

For some of us, it might be easier to muster all our strength for one huge act of devotion. You can count on us in a crisis; we'll come running. But please don't ask us to walk quietly every day to the nursing home to visit. We will gather our courage and speak boldly about Christ before a crowd, but don't expect us to speak to God every morning before work. God, however, cares more for routine faithfulness than sacrifice. *"Your love is like a morning cloud, like the dew that goes away early. . . . For I desire steadfast love and not sacrifice"* (Hosea 6:4,6).

Another obstacle to finishing the race strong in faith is sin. Judy confided that she had an affair in her second year of marriage. She said, "I just couldn't face God, so I stopped going to church and praying." Hebrews 12:1-2 says, *Let us also lay aside every weight and the sin that clings so closely, and let us run with perseverance the race that is set before us, looking to Jesus the pioneer and perfecter of our faith.* We can't let sin block our spiritual progress. Judy learned to accept God's forgiveness. She is healing and growing again.

Although Priscilla witnessed the growth of one of the best New Testament churches at Ephesus, she also saw false doctrine creep into the early church. She heard about the factions and problems erupting in the Christian community at Corinth. She may have been alive to hear about the martyrdom of Paul, Peter, and other disciples. But Priscilla was faithful for the distance, and she can give us an example of lifelong loyalty to Christ.

Jesus in Revelation 2:25-26, 28 promised: *Only hold fast to what you have until I come. To everyone who conquers and continues to do my works to the end, I will give authority over the nations. . . . To the one who conquers I will also give the morning star.*

Bonding with Our Sister, Priscilla

Priscilla applied her enterprising spirit as she helped establish the church at Ephesus. In Revelation 2:4-5, Jesus warned Priscilla's congregation about losing their first love. *But I have this against you, that you have abandoned the love you had at first. Remember then from what you have fallen; repent, and do the works you did at first.*

We can heed that same warning as we endure in our enterprising faith. Make two columns on a sheet of paper. Label one FIRST LOVE. In this column, write down as many details as you can remember of your best, most fulfilling days as a Christian. (What did you do, think, feel, wonder, discover?) Label the other column TODAY'S LOVE. Write down all the characteristics of your love for Christ as it shows itself today. Are there any items in the first column you can repeat this week to renew your first love?

A Prayer for Priscilla's Enterprising Faith

Lord, thank you for Priscilla's enduring faith. Help me stick with the enterprises I know are according to your will. Make me willing to be a team player and an encourager. Keep my love fresh. Amen.

Women Who Were Doers

Tabitha
Lois
The Mother of Rufus

Now in Joppa there was a disciple whose name was Tabitha, which in Greek is Dorcas. She was devoted to good works and acts of charity. (Acts 9:36)

Paul went on also to Derbe and to Lystra, where there was a disciple named Timothy, the son of a Jewish woman who was a believer; but his father was a Greek. He was well spoken of by the believers in Lystra and Iconium. (Acts 16:1-2)

I am reminded of your sincere faith, a faith that lived first in your grandmother Lois and your mother Eunice and now, I am sure, lives in you. (2 Timothy 1:5)

Greet Rufus, chosen in the Lord; and greet his mother— a mother to me also. (Romans 16:13)

34

∞

Tabitha, or Dorcas, A Doer

Tabitha, A Disciple

Now in Joppa there was a disciple whose name was Tabitha, which in Greek is Dorcas. She was devoted to good works and acts of charity (Acts 9:36). The Greek word for disciple used here to describe Tabitha is *mathetria*, a female disciple. This is the only time the word is used in the New Testament. Tabitha was a follower of Christ, and many women since have followed her example of doing good works and acts of charity. Women all over the world have formed Dorcas societies to help the poor.

Tabitha, which means gazelle or pleasant creature, is an example of what James calls a doer. *But be doers of the word, and not merely hearers who deceive themselves* (James 1:22). Tabitha seems to have been a single woman, possibly wealthy, living in Joppa. Joppa was the ancient seaport where Jonah took a ship to sail for Tarshish. In this town overlooking the Mediterranean, there would have been many widows who needed help. Flimsy wooden boats often shipwrecked at sea, and tides carried bodies of seafaring men to the shores of Joppa.

Tabitha did something to meet the needs around her. Luke says that she was *devoted to good works and acts of charity*. When Tabitha died, the loss of her was felt so strongly that people in Joppa sent two men on the twelve-mile walk to Lydda to get Peter. When Peter arrived, the widows cried and showed him the tunics and other clothing that

Tabitha had made while she was with them. Those who grieved for Tabitha didn't have to tell Peter how much Tabitha had done for them. They could show what she had done. Tabitha left tangible evidence of her work.

Although making clothes for poor widows wasn't as glamourous as Peter's mission, Tabitha was honored by one of the greatest miracles in the New Testament. Just as Jesus had raised Jairus' daughter with the words *Talitha cum*, now Peter raised Tabitha with the words *Tabitha cum—Get up!* or *Arise!*

After Peter resurrected Tabitha, her influence increased. *Then she opened her eyes, and seeing Peter, she sat up. He gave her his hand and helped her up. Then calling the saints and widows, he showed her to be alive. This became known throughout Joppa, and many believed in the Lord* (Acts 9:40-42).

Today's Doers

Every community has a few good women who, like Tabitha, are the doers. Everyone counts on these hard workers. Joan is a retired school teacher living in a small midwestern community. She does most of her doing anonymously. When she hears of somebody in trouble, she sends anonymous cards of encouragement or mails a special toy for a child. When someone dies, or is in the hospital, Joan and another friend take turns providing meals long after most people have forgotten about the need.

Martha of Bethany was another doer. She worked hard to prepare for her guests. She served meals to Jesus and his disciples more than once. Because Martha was willing to work hard, Jesus had the nearest thing to a home when he visited there.

We know we need to help others, but in the hectic affairs of life we may put off doing what we know we should. Vicky is raising three stepchildren, cleaning office buildings at night, and selling over the phone during the day. She explained her struggle to be a doer. "I couldn't knit or buy mittens and hats. I couldn't afford time off work to help clean up a neighborhood." For several years, the guilt of not doing the things she thought she should do paralyzed her.

Finally," she continued, "I chose one thing. My family and I sponsor a child in Rwanda with a pledge, letters, and gifts. It's not enough, but it's something I've been able to stick with no matter how busy I get." Vicky became a doer by starting small—selecting one deed she could reasonably complete.

Jesus told the disciples at the Last Supper, *"If you know these things, you are blessed if you do them"* (John 13:17). The blessing is in the doing. We shouldn't become doers out of guilt but because of a heart that breaks with the things that break God's heart. Our gratitude for what God has done for us overflows. We want to please God and give to others in response to God's love. God could accomplish every act of doing without us, but we would be the ones to miss the blessing of doing. Tabitha did not miss the blessing. She used her enterprise to help those who were in need. If we follow her example, we too will become doers.

Bonding with Our Sister, Tabitha

Tabitha made time to do what she could to help others. List at least ten loving acts you would do if you had all the time in the world. Order your list by priority. This week do at least one thing on your list.

35

Lois, A Godly Grandmother

Lois and Her Grandson

Lois was the grandmother of Paul's disciple, Timothy. Her influence reached the early churches and extends even to us today. Yet only
one verse in the Bible mentions her directly: *I am reminded of your sincere
faith, a faith that lived first in your grandmother Lois and your mother Eunice and
now, I am sure, lives in you* (2 Timothy 1:5). This is the only place in the
New Testament where the word *grandmother* appears. Lois's influence
filtered through her daughter Eunice and her grandson Timothy.

Lois's family lived in Lystra (modern Turkey). The colony had
been established by the Roman Emperor Augustus. As a Jewish
woman, Lois raised her daughter, Eunice, to believe in the God of
Israel. Judaism didn't provide women with an advanced education.
The Greco-Roman society in Lystra would have reserved rhetorical
and philosophical training for men. Yet Lois studied the scriptures
and passed them on to her daughter. She was enterprising in her
relationships and her influence on her family.

On Paul's second missionary journey, he met Lois's grandson
Timothy in Lystra. Timothy was a believer, already well spoken of by
other believers. Paul thought so highly of this young, half-Gentile
that he wanted Timothy to travel with him. Lois and Eunice had
raised a godly man. Paul gave much of the credit for Timothy's faithfulness to Lois and Eunice. They had shared their sincere faith with

him. Paul wrote Timothy, *But as for you, continue in what you have learned and firmly believed, knowing from whom you learned it, and how from childhood you have known the sacred writings that are able to instruct you for salvation through faith in Christ Jesus* (2 Timothy 3:14-15). Lois and Eunice had been teaching the scriptures to Timothy since childhood!

Lois helped equip Timothy to become one of the most influential leaders of the early church. It must have been hard for Eunice and Lois to send Timothy off with Paul. But Timothy proved his faithfulness. Paul told the Philippians, *I have no one like him [Timothy] who will be genuinely concerned for your welfare. . . . But Timothy's worth you know, how like a son with a father he has served with me in the work of the gospel* (Philippians 2:20, 22).

Timothy traveled with Paul and was sent on the most delicate assignments. His name is listed with Paul's as a sender of letters to the Corinthians (2 Corinthians 1:1), the Thessalonians (1 Thessalonians 1:1, 2 Thessalonians 1:1), Philemon (1), the Colossians (1:1), and the Philippians (1:1).

Paul wrote two personal letters to Timothy, one from prison when he was close to death. 2 Timothy begins, *To Timothy, my beloved child* (2 Timothy 1:2). Eunice and Lois prepared Timothy and then let him go. They leave us a rich example of an enterprising mother and grandmother.

Today's Enterprising Grandmothers

What can we do for our children and grandchildren, our nieces and nephews, or any other young people God puts in our lives? How can we influence them for Christ as Lois did?

I met eight-year-old Misha when I interviewed her second-grade class in an inner city school. "What's a grandmother?" I asked her. "It's what Mama's going to be when she grows up," Misha answered. "And how about you?" I asked. Misha grew quiet, as if the idea hadn't occurred to her. Then she grinned, "I get to be like Grandma, too!"

Several of Misha's classmates talked about grandmothers who took them to church, waited for them after school, told them Bible stories at bedtime. Their Christian heritage was coming to them through their grandmothers.

Tracy's grandmother died, but her influence lives on. "My grandmother was a storyteller. When I was young, I'd listen to her tell stories about relatives I'd never met. I learned some of my greatest lessons in life from what my grandmother told me about their mistakes and their right decisions."

If we follow Lois's example we will teach our children and grandchildren the scriptures. Lois would have known the commands in Deuteronomy 6:6-9 to keep the commandments and *talk about them when you are at home and when you are away, when you lie down and when you rise.*

Gina remembers how her grandmother used to quote verses to her. "She seemed to know the whole Bible! And everywhere—on mirrors, refrigerators, dashboards—she had verses stuck up. Some of them I've never forgotten."

Lois and Eunice leave us a rich example of a godly heritage extended through the maternal line of spiritual women. One of the greatest, most natural influences we can have is through our connection with the children and grandchildren in our lives. As Lois did, we can extend our influence for Christ through generations.

Bonding with Our Sisters, Lois and Eunice

God gave Lois a tremendous job by entrusting her with her grandson Timothy's spiritual development. Think about your own grandmothers and how they have influenced you directly or indirectly. Thank God for the way God has blessed you through your grandmothers and their children, your parents. If you are a grandmother or a mother, list the children and grandchildren God has entrusted to you. (If you don't have children of your own, name children God has placed within your sphere of influence.) Beside each name, list at least three ways you can extend a godly influence. Be specific (call on Thursdays to let him know I'm praying for him, pick her up after school on Tuesday, share my own spiritual struggles). Follow through with your list this week.

36

∞

The Mother of Rufus

Like a Mother to Me

In the closing of Paul's letter to the Romans, Paul sends an intriguing greeting: *Greet Rufus, chosen in the Lord; and greet his mother—a mother to me also* (Romans 16:13). Paul gives this woman a wonderful tribute. In some way, she had been like a mother to him.

We do not know who Rufus was for certain. For many years scholars speculated that he was the son of Simon of Cyrene, who was forced to carry Jesus' cross at the crucifixion (see Mark 15:21). Whoever Rufus or his mother were, Paul considered the latter as a mother to him. That in itself makes her worth emulating.

We don't know what Rufus' mother did for Paul, but "like a mother" implies giving comfort, encouragement, and unconditional love. Enterprising mothers played a vital role throughout the first century church. When Peter was miraculously freed from King Herod's prison, where did he go? He went where believers were praying for him, to the house of Mary, the mother of John Mark (Acts 12:12). Mark then traveled with Paul and Barnabas to bring the gospel to the early churches.

After Jesus healed Peter's mother-in-law, she rose up immediately to serve them (Luke 4:39). The Syrophoenician woman begged Jesus to heal her daughter, and Jesus praised her faith (Mark 7:24-30). John wrote to *the elect lady and her children, whom I love in the truth, and not only I but also all who know the truth* (2 John 1). The qualities these enterprising mothers showed in persistence, courage, and faith are part of what Paul meant when he said Rufus' mother was like a mother to him.

Today's Women Who Become Like Mothers

What does it mean to be like a mother to someone? There is an African proverb that says, "It takes a whole village to raise a child." The same applies to children of God. If each of us extended protection, comfort, and love to others as Rufus' mother must have done for Paul, God's family would be richer. The world would recognize Christians by their love.

I saw this idea of an extended spiritual family realized in a small mission church in Chicago. Karen studied nights at a city college. Still she found time to look out for Juanita, a thirteen-year-old living with a grandmother and eleven siblings. Karen made sure Juanita stayed in school and did her homework. About the same time, Karen's mother took a ten-year-old girl under her wing. She bought the child school supplies and talked regularly to her about the scriptures. Just as Lois and Eunice influenced Timothy, Karen and her mother changed the lives of several inner-city children.

In the same church, a young couple bought eyeglasses for a neighborhood boy whose mother wouldn't buy them. The women in that small mission church in Chicago were taking the responsibility of acting like mothers to people God brought into their lives.

Unlike Karen and her mother, Janice came from a wealthy neighborhood. When Janice's husband left her with three small children and no money, she found that she too needed someone to be a mother to her. Janice talks about an aunt who came to her rescue during the roughest time in her life. "Aunt Ruth, who lived a few miles from me, took me in with all three kids. She listened to me, but never asked about things I didn't want to talk about." Janice's aunt acted "like a mother" to her.

Rufus' mother had at least two sons of her own, but she took time to treat Paul as a son. She may have done the same for others.

What an honor to have someone write that you were like a mother to him or to her! Rufus' mother kept up the tradition of comfort and caring. We can follow in the same high calling to be "like a mother" to people around us.

Bonding with Our Sister, the Mother of Rufus

List any women who have been "like a mother" to you. What exactly did they do that made them mother-like? (Be as specific as you can.) Write them thank-you letters or call them this week. Try to explain how they were like mothers to you. Ask God to use you in the lives of others. Jot down the names of people you may be able to comfort and encourage in a motherly way. Just as Rufus' mother was like a mother to Paul, we can be like mothers to those people God brings into our lives.

A Prayer for Enterprise and Christian Influence

Dear God, make me the kind of woman whose influence will help your kingdom and your children on earth. Open my eyes so I can see how you're waiting to use me at work, at home, everywhere. Make me like Christ. Fill me with your Spirit that it might over-flow into the lives of others. Thank you for the powerful influence of the women in the New Testament. Amen.

Biblical References Index